Simply Seagrove

An Intimate History of One of Florida's Most Beautiful Beaches

Robert O. Reynolds

Simply Seagrove

An Intimate History of One of Florida's Most
Beautiful Beaches

Robert O. Reynolds

Emerald Waters Press
Tucson, Arizona

Reynolds, Robert O.
Simply Seagrove: An Intimate History of One of Florida's Most Beautiful
    Beaches

Published by Emerald Waters Press LLC
Tucson, Arizona
www.emeraldwaterspress.com

Printed in the United States Of America

1. Gulf Coast (Fla.) – History
2. Walton County (Fla.) – History
3. Gulf Coast (Fla.) – Social life and customs
4. Walton County (Fla.) – Description and travel
5. Walton County (Fla.) – Social life and customs
6. Florida Panhandle (Fla.) – Description and travel
7. Walton County (Fla.) – Biography
8. Tourism – Florida – Gulf Coast – History

F317.W5R49 2018
975.9'9 - dc23   2018906390

Includes bibliographical references and index.

ISBN 978-1-7322473-0-7

To my parents, William F. and Helen M. Reynolds, who had the vision and the daring to search for new places and find our second home.

Contents

Introduction

This book, as the title suggests, is about Seagrove Beach, a place dear to me and to my family. In it I will give some background on the area and try to explain how Seagrove Beach came to be and how it has developed. I will also give background on my family, explain how we came to live in Seagrove, and describe many of our activities there. I will introduce some of the many plants and animals common in this area, and explain a few of the engaging natural phenomena you are bound to encounter here. Although the history is intended to be accurate and useful, it is not intended to be exhaustive, nor to trace in detail the development of the many other communities along Highway 30-A that grew up on both sides of Seagrove. Also, the subject matter is presented from a personal point of view. It primarily covers the period from when my family started traveling to the Florida Panhandle in the late 1950s until around the year 2000. Although I have continued to vacation in the area and took my own family to Seagrove on regular vacations, this is primarily a story about my youth there. Even though since 1990 I have lived primarily in other parts of the country, I believe that Seagrove Beach is a place that gets in your mind and makes you want to return, as I continue to do for cherished vacations.

The waters of the Gulf as seen from the bluff at Seagrove Beach

One

Chapter 1. Some Background on Seagrove Beach

"Where nature did its best" *(C.H. McGee, Sr.)*

Long before there was a Seagrove Beach, the Florida Panhandle was inhabited by Native Americans for thousands of years. Evidence of the earliest inhabitants comes from a shell mound, or midden, which shows that a cultural group existed in the Mack Bayou area before 2500 BC. During the Woodland Period from about 2500-2000 BC, early tools and shell debris were placed in the mound. After the invention of pottery around 2000 BC, pots and fragments of pottery were also added. As early as 1000-1200 CE a ceremonial society called the Fort Walton Culture inhabited what is now Walton and Okaloosa Counties. This society buried its dead in mounds, and excavation of cemeteries at Point Washington and Hogtown Bayou has provided important details of the culture. From roughly the 1400s to the 1800s the Chatot, Choctaw, Muscogee, Creek, Euchee (also spelled Yuchi), and possibly other peoples inhabited the region. Ponce de Leon is usually credited with being the first European to discover the Florida coast, in 1513. He returned later to try to colonize the area, and the French also established settlements nearby. But both the weather and resistance by Native Americans proved formidable obstacles, and many settlements were destroyed.

Great Britain obtained title to the Gulf Coast in the French and Indian War, which ended in 1763. However, Spain entered the Revolutionary War on the side of France and captured several cities on the Gulf Coast, which led to Britain ceding the area to Spain under the Treaty of 1783. Boundary disputes ensued and factions favoring rule by Spain, independents, and the United States argued and sometimes fought for control. There were even various efforts to combine the panhandle with Alabama. Only with the ratification of a treaty between Spain and the United States in February of 1821, was control finalized and the present boundaries established.

Around 1820, Neill McClendon and other settlers from North Carolina and other points north arrived in what is now Walton County after seeking out new land. Then in 1822 the Florida Territory was organized, and not long after that, in 1824, Walton County was created. It was named after George Walton, Jr., a secretary of the Florida Territory, whose father was a signer of the Declaration of Independence. This was before Florida was granted statehood, which followed in 1845.

The two oldest communities in the area, Point Washington and Grayton Beach, are often referred to as being founded around 1890. However, there are references to activity in Point Washington dating back to the Civil War and earlier. The community developed around a sawmill, which was built to process the abundant yellow pine timber in the area. Point Washington sits at the eastern end of Choctawhatchee Bay, and is about five miles inland from the Gulf. Grayton Beach was founded by Army General William Miller and William Wilson, who moved their families to the area in 1890. They named the community after Charles T. Gray, who had built a homestead in the area about 1885. Originally the beach area was not a desirable place to settle since the inland areas had an abundance of timber and the sandy soil near the coast was not good for farming. But about 1913 W.H. Butler and his son Van, from DeFuniak Springs, bought much of the land and started the difficult task of trying to build a resort area out of the forest.

Warm coastal waters, sugar-white sand and a string of rare inland lakes, called coastal dune lakes, made the area beautiful and provided many opportunities for recreation. The main east-west highway nearest the beaches, US Highway 98, was constructed in the mid 1930s, but getting there from communities to the north wasn't easy. The nearly 30-mile long Choctawhatchee Bay formed a natural barrier to travel to south Walton County and for years it could only be crossed by ferry. But with the completion of a causeway and bridge on US Highway 331 in 1936 there was finally a direct pathway to south Walton County. County road 283 from US 98 to Grayton was also complete by the mid-1930s.

As the United States Department of the Interior Geological Survey map from 1936 shows, Seagrove Beach was already named at that time, and Walton County maps from as early as 1931 show the name. Buts let's go back further in time. Some have claimed that this

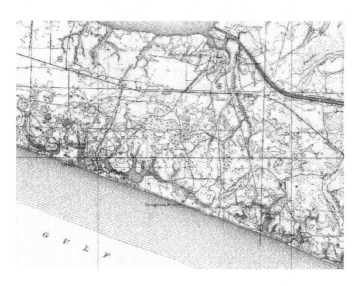

USGS map of Walton County dated 1936 shows the name "Seagrove Beach".

short stretch of beach about two miles east of Grayton Beach is the highest point on the Gulf coast from Key West to Brownsville, Texas. The high bluff, covered with oak trees, was apparently referred to by sea captains as "green hill" and it was a useful navigation tool for them, visible from far out in the Gulf. Another early name for Seagrove Beach was "Russ Hammock" or "Russ's Hammock", as once stated in a letter to the editor of the *Walton Sun* newspaper written by a local resident. A "hammock" in this case, which may also be called a hummock, refers to an area, usually higher than its surroundings, with deep, rich soil and hardwood vegetation. Seagrove Beach, with its high bluff and oak trees, certainly fits this description.

The 160 acres of land that became Seagrove Beach was owned by the United States government until 1904, when President Theodore Roosevelt signed a homestead certificate granting ownership to a private individual. The certificate referenced the Act of Congress approved 20th May, 1862, "To secure Homesteads to actual Settlers on the Public Domain." The land was sold to another individual that

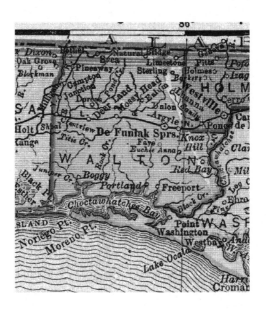

Early Map of a portion of Western Florida showing that the land south of Choctawhatchee Bay was earlier part of Washington County (courtesy of Florida Center for Instructional Technology, University of South Florida).

same year, and interestingly, the indenture describing the sale was certified by a Justice of the Peace named James L. Russ. The surname Russ was common at the time, and there may have been a connection to the earlier Russ's Hammock name. It should be noted that these exchanges took place in Washington County, because the part of South Walton County containing Seagrove Beach was part of Washington County until 1913.

Some references state that the name Seagrove dates from 1923 when the Seagrove Company moved into the area, bought land, and filed a plat map with Walton County. However, F.B. Calloway, later the president of the Seagrove Company, had actually owned the land since 1921, along with his wife and others. Property records show that in 1922 they sold the land to the company, which then drew up a plat dated that year using the name Seagrove, and began selling lots. The original plat is shown in Chapter Four. The company came back and filed a corrected plat in 1923, from which it sold additional lots. At about the same time, a hotel was built near the end of the road that connected the beach to US 98 (now County Road 395), about where it now intersects County Road 30-A. The hotel was apparently popular during the holidays with people from communities to the north, such as Point Washington. Not many lots were sold from the original plat, and the Seagrove Company later filed a revised plat referred to as the First Addition, and began selling lots from that plat. Although several lots were sold during the 1930s and 1940s, not many structures were built on these lots, which were near the intersection of the newly paved road CR 395 and the newer road running along the top of the bluff (now CR 30-A) that extended east about a mile to Eastern Lake. The cover photo was taken looking south along CR 395, and CR 30-A runs left to right near the top. Another subdivision called SeaHighland was platted in 1948 just east of Seagrove.

In 1949 C.H. McGee, Sr., a developer from Panama City, became the new owner of the roughly 160 acres of gulf-front land originally developed by the Seagrove Company. McGee had known about the land for at least 18 months and had made periodic trips to the area along with his son C.H. McGee, Jr., known as Cube, trying to get the company's president at the time, J.R. Moody, to sell it to him. After putting him off time and time again, Moody finally agreed to sell the property for $75,000, and McGee had his start. He decided to keep the name Seagrove Beach, and those trees and the high bluff became his selling points. He began building houses, and started Seagrove Beach Real Estate to sell the homes. He also opened the

C.H. McGee. Sr. and his wife Louise in an undated photo (courtesy of the Seagrove Village Market).

C.H. McGee, Sr.'s Seagrove Beach Real Estate office circa 1949 (courtesy of the Seagrove Village Market).

Seagrove Village Market in 1949, which provided the only place nearby to buy food or gas or to use a pay phone. The market is visible in the cover photo, partially hidden by the trees, where you see the dense group of cars on the right-hand side of the road. During the next two years McGee filed plats for two additions to Seagrove beyond what the Seagrove Company had laid out. After he passed away in 1954, his son Cube took over the development, along with C.H. McGee, Sr.'s wife Louise. The photo shows Cube in front of his real estate sign in the mid-1950s

Cube McGee and the sign for his Seagrove Beach Real Estate office in the mid-1950s (courtesy of the DeFuniak Springs Herald Breeze).

Local resident Philip "Flip" Spann once climbed the water tower that used to be located behind the market (Philip Spann IV, personal communication, May 4, 2018), and he captured the photo on the next page in the 1970s. It shows the area to the right, or West, of the cover photo, and highlights the fact that there was a stretch along the bluff, next to the group of houses at the intersection, where nothing had yet been built. Houses have been built on those vacant lots since that time, but despite a lot of recent teardowns and replacements, several homes shown in the photo are still there today.

The road that became County Road 30-A was later extended to the east along the coast, eventually connecting to US 98 about eight miles east of Seagrove. Even though Grayton Beach was only two miles west of Seagrove, the beach road didn't extend west of the Seagrove area. So to get to Grayton you had to drive up CR 395 to US 98, travel west a couple of miles, and follow CR 283 south to Grayton. The other older beach communities such as Blue Mountain Beach, Dune Allen Beach, and Santa Rosa Beach to the west, and Seacrest to the east, were mostly developed in the 1950s and 1960s, as Seagrove was growing. The beach road, CR 30-A, was eventually extended so that it now runs about 15 miles from the Topsail Preserve area on the west end to Inlet Beach on the east end. The newer communities of Seaside, Watercolor, Rosemary Beach, Watersound, and Alys Beach were developed from the 1980s to the early 2000s, all linked by CR 30-A and the emerald green waters of the Gulf. Several of the noted coastal dune lakes are interspersed with the developments along CR 30-A, and will be discussed in more detail in Chapter Six.

View of CR 30-A taken from the old water tower that once stood behind the
Seagrove Village Market (courtesy of Philip and Flip Spann).

Two

Chapter 2. Our Life at Seagrove and a Story from the Village Market

"The real voyage of discovery consists not in seeking new landscapes but in having new eyes." (Marcel Proust, paraphrase from "Remembrance of Things Past, The Prisoner")

I grew up in Montgomery, Alabama, and like many families from that area in the 1950s and 1960s my parents would take our family to Destin or Fort Walton Beach for vacations. We would go for one or two weeks each summer, and stay at places like the Holiday Inn, Silver Beach Cottages and Hotel, the Spyglass Inn, or the Jack Tar Beach House. Alabama at the time had several very attractive and accessible inland lakes that had been built as part of the push for hydroelectric power generation, and most families who wanted to own a second home for weekends and vacations were building houses there, on Lake Jordan, Lake Martin, or one of the others. But my parents really loved the beach, so they started investigating property in the panhandle. They also both loved to fish, and although the fishing was great in Alabama, the beach area offered more bodies of water and more variety. The photo shows our family after a day on a charter boat operated by Destin captain "Smokey" Jones and his wife Edna.

My family with the day's catch from charter boat "Edna" in Destin circa 1960.

The panhandle was a three-hour drive from Montgomery and many areas were not that well developed, so our trips, mostly arranged by my mother, took a lot of planning. We visited Grayton Beach, Seagrove Beach, Blue Mountain Beach, and Seacrest, among others. Once we rented a house in Seagrove for a week's vacation, a place called Hurricane Hall, and my parents finally decided Seagrove was the place they liked best. It was one of the few places that had any elevation above the water, thanks to the high bluff. Not only did that offer protection during storms, but the views of the water were spectacular. So after many more trips and several months of looking, they finally settled on a house near the intersection of CR 30-A and CR 395, the center of old Seagrove. It was one of the homes originally built in the early 1950s by C.H. McGee, Sr and Cube, in what was called the Seagrove Beach Second Addition. The roof is just visible in the upper left-hand corner of the cover photo, which shows Seagrove as it appeared when driving in from the north. Cube was also the real estate agent handling the sale. The transaction was settled in August of 1962, when I was entering the eighth grade in Montgomery.

We immediately began going down for weekends throughout much of the year, as well as for vacations in the summer. When we went to Seagrove on weekends during the school year my parents would pick up my sister and me at school on Friday afternoons at 3PM and we would drive straight to the house, getting there in time to fix dinner and walk on the beach. We then had all day Saturday, and would leave for home after noon on Sunday. Jacques Cousteau's underwater adventures were all the rage and made us eager to explore the beach and ocean and learn more about the exotic creatures around us. We already knew how inviting the warm waters of the Gulf were, and soon found that walking a short distance on the beach took us to very different sights. Eastern Lake, with its outfall to the Gulf and a different water environment, was about a mile to the east. And two miles to the west was Grayton Beach with its little store and quaint

The house my parents bought in Seagrove Beach in 1962.

paths. That was often a good nighttime walk for us kids. We had books like Rachel Carson's *The Sea Around Us* and Henry Beston's *The Outermost House* on the bookshelves, and so even when the weather was bad we were steeped in the lore of the beach and the ocean.

We soon met families from Birmingham, Greenville, and Dothan, Alabama, as well as others from Montgomery. Several of the families included kids our age, so we always had friends to share activities with. We also became acquainted with some people who had retired to the area, like John Fonville, and they were always friendly and a wonderful source of both information and sometimes tools or other things we needed to borrow.

As you read in Chapter One, C.H. McGee, Sr. had opened the Seagrove Village Market when he developed the area, and since it was located on CR 395 about a block north of the intersection with CR 30-A, it was a short walk from our house. So when we arrived on a Friday evening, if there was a food item we hadn't brought or picked

The Seagrove Village Market in the 2000s. Cube's "Seagrove on the Beach Real Estate" office is on the left (Florida State Archives Photographic Collection).

up on the way my mother would send me to the Village Market to get it. Since we went down regularly, I made lots of trips there and got to know the place pretty well.

Like many boys in the 1960s I developed an interest in coin collecting, searching my and my parents' change looking for dates and mint marks of Lincoln pennies, Jefferson nickels, and so forth. There was lots of interest in coins at the time and some interesting developments. A new engraving of the Lincoln Memorial had been added to the reverse side of the Lincoln penny in 1959, marking the first permanent change in 50 years, and Congress authorized a new design for half dollars shortly after President Kennedy's death in 1963. Also, dimes, quarters, and half dollars were still made of silver in the early 60s, but as the supply of silver began to dwindle, the United States Treasury stopped using it in most coins after 1964, making the silver coins more desirable. I never had access to any sources of change other than regular stores when in Montgomery, and, of course, I also looked at my change while in Florida.

As I remember, most times I went to the Village Market on weekends and evenings the store was staffed by a man named J.O. Thornton, who I understand was originally from Prattville, Alabama, near Montgomery. I was often the only customer in the store and since I saw him often enough I would strike up a conversation while shopping. He told me about his son and I commented about my family. I don't remember how it occurred, whether he saw me looking at my change or whether I saw him get some extra change from storage. Or maybe I mentioned that I was into coins, but somehow we got on the subject, and he asked if I was looking for anything in particular. I explained that I didn't have any favorites but was looking for dates I didn't have or that I knew were hard to find. Anyway, at one point he told me to hold on for a minute. He bent down and opened a low cabinet behind the register and slowly pulled out some old-style cigar boxes. He put them on the counter and opened them up. They were mostly half dollars, which at the time, just before the Kennedy half dollars were issued, were called Liberty Walking half dollars. Now for a kid in junior high school with a small allowance and other things to buy, collecting quarters and half dollars got expensive in a hurry. I didn't have many of those, and certainly not any that were hard to find. But I knew from reading coin books what the desirable ones were, and quickly noticed that he had a few of them. He wasn't saving them for any special purpose though, and I remember he actually agreed to let me take the box home, go through it to find the ones I wanted, and then bring it back and pay him for what I had taken. After looking through the boxes it turned out he had many of the scarcer dates from the 1910s and 1920s, dates I might never have found in my normal travels. And they were all dates still made of silver! It was almost like finding a coin collection someone was dumping, except I only paid face value for each coin. Quite an exciting event for a teenager just going to the grocery store! Mr. Thornton eventually left the store and it became much busier as Seagrove developed, but I'll always remember those quieter days and my friend J.O. Thornton.

Three

Chapter 3. Jeeps on the Beach

"Wha's a Jeep?" Popeye   *(Elzie C. Segar, "Thimble Theatre")*

My father knew from talking to Cube McGee that you could take vehicles like a Jeep on the beach, since Cube had one that he used to launch his fishing boat from the beach in front of his house. He also knew from his time in World War II that Jeeps were one of the most versatile vehicles ever built. The husband of an employee in my father's office in Montgomery, who was a lieutenant in the fire department by trade, spent a lot of time working on vehicles and was an expert. So my father arranged for him to buy a used Jeep in Montgomery and rebuild and modify it for use at the beach. The model was a 1950 Willys, probably a model CJ-3A, the civilian version of the original military models. "CJ" apparently stood for "Civilian Jeep", but the origin of the original term "Jeep" is less certain. Apparently, the first use of the name in print to describe the military vehicle was by the journalist Katherine Hillyer in the *Washington Daily News* in February, 1941, and it appeared again in 1942 in an article in *Scientific American*. A common theory is that the word was derived from the initials GP, which stood for "General Purpose". But according to sources, the G actually stood for Government and the P represented a certain size vehicle, and the full acronym included W, which stood for the Willys Company, one of the manufacturers of the vehicle. And the word Jeep was already in use well before the GPW acronym was created. In 1919 cartoonist E.C. Segar introduced a comic strip entitled *Thimble Theatre*, and in 1929 a one-eyed, pipe-smoking, spinach-eating hero named Popeye made his debut in the strip. Then in 1936 a magical teleporting dog named "Eugene the Jeep" was introduced and became Popeye's sidekick. Some theorize that soldiers adopted the name because of the vehicle's ability to go just about anywhere, just like Eugene the Jeep. Another theory claims the name derived from World War I slang in which a jeep was a new recruit, and the World War II Jeep was a new, unproven vehicle. Whatever the true origin of the name, the Jeep is now a name and a vehicle recognized the world over.

Now setting a vehicle up for driving on sand involved more than the obvious items like installing wider tires and rims. Since the vehicles would sometimes be driven through salt water and always be exposed to salt spray, all metal parts were subject to rust and corrosion. For fenders and floor boards that wasn't necessarily a show-stopper, but steel tubing used for the brake lines was another story. You could try to rinse off the bottom of the vehicle with a garden hose after each use, but that wasn't fool proof, and not good enough for the brakes. A rusted brake line could lead to disaster if it developed a leak when you needed to stop quickly. So all the factory brake lines with their fittings and brackets had to be removed and replaced with copper tubing, which would not rust. This Jeep version didn't have a roof or doors and windows, but he fitted it with a canvas top so it would be more comfortable in sun or rain. If the weather was good we would take the top off, and you could also tilt the windshield forward onto the hood for a really breezy ride.

When the Jeep was finally ready and after we test drove it in Montgomery, we drove it to Seagrove in the summer, and were finally ready to have full mobility on the beach. The big day came; I drove it down the road to a place where there was no bluff and with access to the beach, and promptly got stuck in the sand. It wasn't that the tires were dug in – instead, I just couldn't get the vehicle to move. You see, all older Jeeps had a manual transmission and clutch, and getting it started in soft sand took some experience and technique with the clutch. Just revving the engine and popping the clutch wasn't very practical and often would just spin the tires and dig a hole. And without enough engine speed it would stall. So we walked back to the house and called Cube for help. Cube had lots of experience on that beach, and his Jeep was set up really well, with extremely wide rims and wide slick tires. He knew from experience that a slick tire would work as well as or better than a treaded tire under those conditions, and he also had lots of experience driving in the sand, even in extreme situations like towing and launching a boat in the surf. But although his Jeep had tires better suited for the sand, he took one look at our Jeep and said it was fine, once I learned how to drive it in those conditions. He patiently showed me how to feather the clutch and adjust the throttle to start in sand. It took some practice, but after a while I was driving like a pro. The photo shows me in 1966 driving on CR 30-A. Note the significant rust on the front fender and left side, evidence of the action of the salt water and spray.

The author in the Jeep in 1966.

Once you had a jeep in the area, there were lots of fun places to go with it. After a while we met other people with Jeeps, and sometimes we kids would form a little 'caravan' of Jeeps. The dirt roads north of CR 30_A in Seagrove, like Grove St. and Forest St., were a shady place to go, and dirt roads into the Point Washington State Forest off CR 395 and CR 30-A provided great areas to explore. You could also get into dunes just west of Seagrove where CR 30-A ended, or near Eastern Lake and points farther east. The beach was still a favorite place to drive, but getting down there was not trivial (even when you knew how to drive in sand!) because of the high bluff at Seagrove Beach with its elevation of almost 40 feet. You could drive a mile or so down to Eastern Lake where there was no bluff, but that meant driving back up the beach to Seagrove again if you wanted to get near the front of the house, so we usually preferred a closer access point. That access was a crude sort of road, what you might call a 'Jeep trail' that had been cut into the bluff near where Hinton Drive is today.

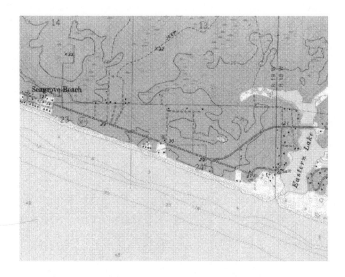

USGS Topographic map from 1970 showing location of jeep trail. At the center of the photo you can see a dotted path that juts below the main road (CR 30-A). The depression to the left of the path was probably our trail down the bluff to the beach.

I don't have a closeup photo from that time, but looking at a modern map, it might have been where there is a small stream emptying into the Gulf, shown on the 1970 map as a small depression extending from the beach up to CR 30-A. That trail was closer than going to Eastern Lake, but it took an experienced driver to drive the trail uphill. The pathway had some curve, the sand was very loose and deep, and there was a drop-off into a hole on one side. If you approached the path going too slowly you'd bog down in the deep sand, come to a stop, and never be able to get started again. But just building up a lot of speed wouldn't do it either because with the curves in the path you'd run the risk of falling off the side. It took a delicate combination of enough approach speed, a steady hand on the wheel negotiating the curves, and just enough throttle to keep your momentum going up the slope. Always a little scary but lots of fun and very satisfying when you did it right. Now that I knew how to drive on the beach and we had the nearby access point, it was possible to keep the Jeep on the beach in front of the house and take off from there. Great for picnics and carrying a lot of beach gear. And with some experience you could launch a boat from a trailer directly into the Gulf. That did involve driving down to Eastern Lake so you had a relatively flat path from the road to the beach for the Jeep towing the trailer. And once you got onto the beach, launching was still no easy task because to get the trailer far enough into the water for the boat to float, the tires of the Jeep almost certainly had to be in the water, where the sand could be very soft. But with practice we were able to do it. We could also launch the boat in the lake and explore and fish. If the channel from Eastern Lake to the Gulf was open, we could go back and forth between the two, a lot easier than having to launch separately in each body of water. All in all, the combination of the beach and the Jeep, sometimes with a boat added, really opened up the possibilities for fun.

As more families bought Jeeps, gatherings at times got larger, and at some point groups both met on the beach, and staged parades on the paved road to celebrate the Fourth of July. The parades often continued to the western boundary of Seagrove Beach and were met by a similar group from Grayton Beach.

Jeeps gathered for the Fourth of July on the beach at Seagrove circa the 1980s
(photo courtesy of Philip and Flip Spann).

By the 1970s, small sailboats were also popular, especially catamarans like the "Hobie Cat", that offered stability when sailing in a large body of water like the Gulf. Access to the beach via Jeeps meant the sailboats could be trailered to the beach and left in front of the owners' homes. The story goes that some Hobie owners in Grayton Beach got the idea in 1981 to have a race from Grayton to Seagrove Beach. They figured they could charge a $20 entry fee and reward each captain and crew member with a t-shirt and a beer at the finish. Since Grayton Beach residents thought of themselves as poor, they went by the nickname 'rags'. And since everyone in Seagrove was better off, they were called 'riches'. So the first race was called the "Rags to Riches Regatta". The next year the course was reversed, sailing from Seagrove to Grayton, so they called it Riches to Rags. The race was a success for several years, and varying conditions in the Gulf guaranteed to keep things interesting. On at least one occasion a Hobie was flipped stern-over-bow by the waves, and on another a boat was disabled far from shore and the sailors not rescued until the following day. The last consecutive annual race was held in 1992, and no events were organized until a few enthusiasts managed to bring it back starting in 2009. The 21st running occurred on July 1, 2017, and a 2018 regatta is advertised online for June 30, 2018.

The running of the "Rags to Riches Regatta" at Seagrove circa the 1980s (photo courtesy of Philip and Flip Spann).

four

Chapter 4. Some Customs, Some Restrictions, and Some Disputes

"A bad agreement is better than a good lawsuit." *(Italian Proverb)*

As mentioned in Chapter One, the Seagrove Company first submitted a plat map for Seagrove in 1922, which was replaced with a revised plat named Seagrove First Addition in 1939. When C.H. McGee, Sr. arrived in 1949, he filed another addition to the original layout, and the next year another. Both of these additions extended along the bluff overlooking the beach east of the original plats, and also included lots on the streets extending inland. C.H. McGee, Jr., "Cube", built a house in the first of these additions, overlooking the Gulf. That road along the bluff was later designated CR 30-A, and when C.H. McGee, Sr. and Cube built the houses on the south side of the road, overlooking the water, they also built a four-foot-wide walkway right near the edge of the bluff. This was kind of a sidewalk, where you wouldn't expect to find a sidewalk, and it formed a natural connecting path between the houses that encouraged walking along the bluff from house to house. We had a large palm tree in front of our house, which leaned out toward the Gulf, almost over the walkway, as shown in the photo. Birmingham businessman Elton Stephens had been one of the early buyers of lots along the bluff, and he and his wife Alys mounted a ship's bell on a pole next to the walk. That was probably the best way to signal people down on the beach so they could hear it above the sound of the wind and surf. Other homeowners put out chairs or benches, and we used to visit our neighbors in the evening after dinner, in sharp contrast to he privacy walls and hedges that you often see today. McGee also wanted to make sure people had access to the beach, even those that didn't own Gulf-front homes, so he provided for an easement for a walkway and steps to the beach about every fifth house along the bluff. The walkway along the top connected all these steps so it was easy not only to visit neighbors but also to go up and down to the water at any point along the beach.

The walkway along the top of the bluff connecting some of the early homes in Seagrove Beach. Note the ship's bell that neighbors Elton and Alys Stephens placed next to the walk.

McGee was determined to create a tidy and pleasant community, so he included various rules and restrictions when selling his lots. Restrictions in the deeds strictly controlled the number of stories and square footage of the homes, and the position of a house on the lot. And no residential lot could contain more than two dwelling units. The construction materials were also controlled, with a list of approved materials for the walls and another for the roofs. For the First through Third Addition deeds prohibited sewage or garbage from being discharged into the Gulf of Mexico or deposited on any property dedicated for parks, streets or avenues. Instead sewage had to be disposed of in septic tanks and underground water disposal systems. A clause directed that "no noxious activities, offensive noises or odors, nor any nuisance will be permitted on any of the above said properties". No outdoor privy (outhouse) was permitted on any lot and each lot owner was required to provide for sanitary garbage container and disposal. Those seem like prudent restrictions, and probably applied to other properties in the area. However, as early as 1953, another restriction was included on at least some lots for the First Addition. It read "Not any of said property shall be sold, leased or rented to, or occupied by any person or persons other than the Caucasian race, but domestic servants or other races actually employed by those residing on said property may reside thereon while thus employed". Some of the deeds permitted building one garage or garage apartment on each lot in addition to the dwelling, and many of the homes had such garages, or carports, with a separate guest house built as part of the carport. These guest houses were often called 'servant's quarters', and owners would sometimes bring their housekeepers along for a summer vacation. I remember when my parents brought a housekeeper with us from Montgomery for a week's vacation. She helped my mother with cleaning and kitchen work during the day, and then socialized with other housekeepers in the evening. She also spiffed up her little apartment just the way she liked it, and was thrilled to have a trip to the beach. Incidentally, McGee's restriction concerning race was not exactly unprecedented. The subdivision called SeaHighland, which borders Seagrove Beach to the east, contained a restriction from 1948 that read "No part of said land or any interest therein shall be given, loaned, leased, rented, encumbered or conveyed to or occupied by any person of Negro Blood, except that this restriction shall not prevent any occupant from keeping and maintaining on the lot such servant, white or colored, as may be required for family use." That and other restrictions were to run until 1980, when they would automatically renew for successive ten-year periods unless voted down by the owners.

Restrictions addressing how the land between the residential lots and the Gulf would be used were included on some of the legal documents such as plat maps, and the subject has been debated and even litigated on more than one occasion. I ran across the public record of a District Court of Appeal ruling concerning a lawsuit filed in 1985 by a homeowner named Marie S. Flowers, along with others, naming Seagrove Beach, Inc. as defendant. Seagrove Beach, Inc. was the name of the company Cube McGee and his father started after his father originally bought the land from the Seagrove Company. The plaintiffs in the case wanted certain land to be dedicated for use only as a public park and not developed. The lawsuit referred to the original plat filed by the Seagrove Company in 1923, and noted that the plat and its associated dedication dedicated certain property between the adjoining highway and the Gulf of Mexico as a public park. The plaintiffs had bought property based on provisions of that plat, but there were several complications.

The first complication was that the dedication of land as a park was apparently never accepted by the Walton County government and the land was never used by the public as a park. Also, according to the court ruling no lots were ever sold with explicit reference to that plat. In fact, the Seagrove Company's board of directors later decided to cancel that original plan and so had the subdivision resurveyed in 1939. They filed a new plat entitled "Seagrove First Addition" which made no reference to a park and specifically excluded that land from the development. The company stockholders later showed approval by ratifying the board's action. The revised plat on file with Walton

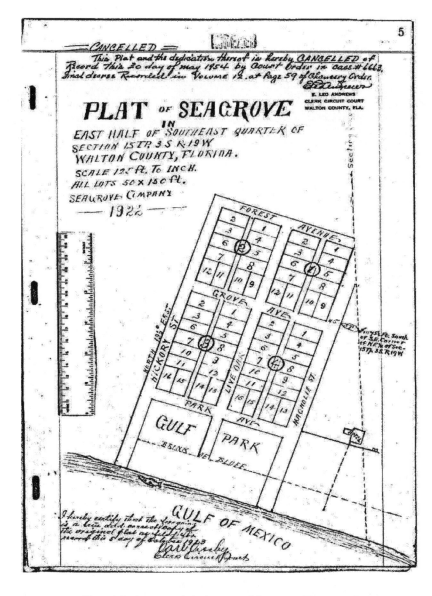

The original unrecorded plat map of Seagrove. The second page was called the "Dedication" and contained stipulations as to the use of the land. Plaintiffs in the lawsuit never saw this plat but claimed that some of its stipulations should be enforced regarding land they later purchased (Walton County, Florida).

County doesn't show any land dedicated as a park, but there might be an indication of what had gone on before because the road that is now called CR 30-A was shown as "Park Ave.".

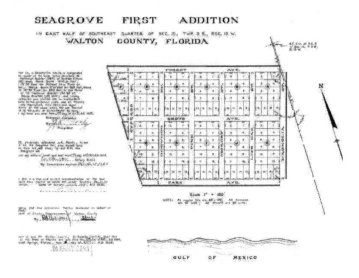

Plat map of Seagrove Beach First Addition from 1939 with no mention of a park (Walton County, Florida).

Flowers, the plaintiff in the lawsuit, bought lots in 1943 and 1944 according to the revised plat (with no park), and had never been shown the original 1923 plat. But she claimed that the salesman (since deceased) had promised verbally that the area in dispute was and would remain a park, with no construction permitted on it. And she backed that claim up with the fact that the property owners had been allowed to use the land as a picnic area and playground from the time she purchased her property until 1981. The other plaintiffs had similar stories.

Apparently everything went along fine until 1981, when the company decided to sell a 60' section of the disputed property, resulting in was the lawsuit. Both the trial court and later an appeals court ruled that the land could be sold, finding that the company's original offer in 1923 to dedicate some land as a park had been withdrawn before the County accepted it. The appeals court also described some requirements of common law and ruled that there had been no common law dedication of the park by public use, and that no use inconsistent with private ownership had ever been allowed. The court elaborated on its decision by stating that the plaintiffs never saw the 1923 plat, the one that was later replaced, showing a park. The decision stated that the owners' argument that the newer 1939 plat was merely an extension of the 1923 document, so that reference to the newer plat was equivalent to referring to the older one, was not persuasive. Although the plaintiff claimed that the salesman had originally promised orally that the disputed area would remain a park, the appeals court found that because so much time had passed since that sale, and since the salesman had passed away in the interim, the trial court was justified in not accepting the plaintiff's argument. Finally the court said that even though the Seagrove Company had allowed some limited construction on the disputed land, that construction was permitted only on special easements and did not preclude the company from now selling the land. Although I assume

1949 aerial photo showing the Seagrove area around the time C.H. McGee, Sr. purchased the development. Western Lake is at upper left, CR 395 comes down from the top, CR 30-A goes left to right, and the development of Seahighland is at the lower right. The fuzzy area in the center includes the 1922 park (USGS).

the ruling was made with all available information and will stand, I uncovered some interesting facts in my research on this subject. First, I have found records of land sales referring to the original plat, both in 1922 and in 1923. Also, not only did the original plat, dated 1922 by the Seagrove Company and filed on October 1, 1923, show and dedicate land as a public park, but some property sales explicitly referred to the park. In some cases the deed to a piece of land assured the buyer that no structures would ever be built on the so-called Gulf Park, granting the buyer "the right to prevent and restrain the construction of any buildings on the said lands adjacent to said lot, marked on said plat as "Gulf Park", and on lands between said park and the Gulf of Mexico". Curiously, I found that most, if not all, of the early buyers later sold the lots back to the Seagrove Company, so maybe that's why the original company was able to submit the new plat in 1939 and have it recorded, enabling the later company to prevail in the Flowers lawsuit. The 1949 aerial photo above shows the Seagrove area around the time C.H. McGee, Sr. purchased the development, after the Seagrove Company had re-plated the original layout and apparently repurchased some lots from buyers. The fuzzy area at the center includes the land that was originally designated as a park in 1922, but later re-platted and sold as lots. I find it interesting that the other features on the map appear sharp, but that particular area is fuzzy enough to make it hard to discern any detail. Even the road, what is now CR 30-A, is clear and sharp to the right of the intersection, and clear to the left of the fuzzy patch, but disappears entirely in the center. And that contrast between sharp features elsewhere and the fuzzy area near the intersection was not limited to just this series of photos. It persisted on aerial photos taken from as early as 1941 to photos taken in 1956. The reader can make his or her own judgment as to what took place there back in Seagrove's early days.

A somewhat similar controversy arose after the beach and bluff were damaged in the record setting hurricane season of 2005. Faced with bluff erosion more severe than most owners had ever seen, there was an immediate drive to build some sort of protection for the bluff, presumably in the form of sea walls. The Florida Department of Environmental Protection (DEP) issued an emergency order that allowed private property owners to take steps to protect eligible structures from further damage. There were a number of conditions to be met and further steps in the future, but many homeowners were willing to do whatever was necessary. Several designs were proposed, and Walton County issued emergency construction permits for a short time, which many homeowners purchased. Contracts were signed with local contractors and some of the designs were built, but only later were the subjects of ownership and maintenance fully examined. Although the permits had allowed building of the seawalls on the 'seaward' side of the bluff, they did not address the question of ownership. The original DEP order allowed the seawalls to be built, but they were considered temporary, and could only remain in place if the owner then applied to the DEP for what was called a Coastal Construction Control Line permit. Back around the 1980s or 1990s the state had determined that in order to help protect the beach and dunes it would limit construction of private structures by establishing a control line defining how close to the beach property owners could build. For the seawalls the DEP was willing to let the structures violate the control line limit, but only if they met several other requirements. Regarding the question of ownership, many owners probably thought they owned the bluff and possibly part of the beach, but an examination of the plat maps of Seagrove Second and Third Additions shows that the land below the top of the bluff was marked "Dedicated for Swimming Park", so Gulf-front lots ended at the top of the bluff. These two plat additions cover all the Gulf front lots in Seagrove from Live Oak St. west of CR 395 all the way to what used to be The Seagrove Villas Hotel, and where the neighborhood of Seahighland starts. The land from the top of the bluff to the Gulf belongs to Walton County, not the homeowners. Thus, in many cases it was only during the permit application and review process that homeowners discovered that the seawalls they had built were not on their property, but rather on land owned by the County.

Plat map of Seagrove Third Addition showing the land designated for public use (Walton County, Florida).

Some of the Gulf front lots in the original Seagrove development do extend to the high tide line of the Gulf, as do some lots in other subdivisions in the area. Since the DEP required homeowners to get the permission of the property owner for seawalls not on their property, the homeowners were forced to negotiate with Walton County for permission to keep their walls on County property. After discussion between homeowners and the County, the County wrote a "Coastal Armoring License Agreement", and the homeowners with seawalls were given a chance to obtain County approval so they could keep the walls in place. Although this solved one problem for the homeowners, it came with many additional conditions. The owner was required to pay an annual lease fee to the County for use of the property on which the seawall had been built, to obtain all other applicable permits, to maintain the seawall, to make any future modifications the County might request, to have the wall inspected by a licensed engineer twice a year, and to file a report with the County. Some protection from Mother Nature was obtainable, but it was neither cheap nor easy.

This controversy is somewhat reminiscent of a land use case in Okaloosa County that made it all the way to the United States

Supreme Court in 2010. In that case the state wanted to renourish some eroded beach in the Destin area by placing more sand on it, and to make it accessible to all citizens. But some of the beachfront property owners preferred to opt out of the arrangement, declaring they would rather have a beach that was narrow and eroded, but private, than have a wide beach that was public. Much discussion failed to solve the impasse, so six Destin property owners sued, under the name "Stop the Beach Renourishment, Inc.". The case ultimately was heard by the United States Supreme Court, which ruled that the state did have the authority to rebuild its beaches, and that those beaches would then be considered public.

five

Chapter 5. The Old Community of Point Washington and the 'Haunted House'

"What terrified me will terrify others; and I need only describe the spectre which had haunted my midnight pillow." (Mary Shelley, "Frankenstein, Or the Modern Prometheus", Introduction)

One short Jeep caravan trip my friends and I liked was to drive up CR395 to the main highway, US 98, cross the highway, and continue on CR395 to the old community of Point Washington. Originally founded to harvest the timber in the area, it dates back to about 1890, the period when Grayton Beach was founded. Point Washington sits at the eastern tip of Choctawhatchee Bay, which visitors from many parts of Florida, Alabama, and points north cross to get to the beaches. Going to the north end of CR395 took us to the shore of Tucker Bayou, with a little beach area, a short wooden pier, and a boat ramp for launching into the bay. The mostly dirt roads leading off either side of the highway provided fun exploring under the oak and pine trees. There was an old school house, a tiny post office, a very old cemetery, and at one time a ferry across the Intracoastal Waterway. The Waterway, described further in Chapter Six, was completed in the mid-1930s, and once it was built, the only quick way to get to communities north or east of Point Washington was by a ferry that ran from just east of Point Washington across to the community of Bunker. The small ferry could hold one or two vehicles and was operated by a cable that could be lowered into the water for boats to pass. It operated until sometime in the 1980s.

The Bunker Ferry in Point Washington circa 1985 (photo courtesy of Alice Forrester).

If you knew which road to drive into the woods and where to look, you could see the remains of an old house we called the "haunted house". The setting was beautiful, with giant live oak trees covered with Spanish moss hanging from their branches. I don't remember how much we learned about the old house at the time. But it turns out that our "haunted house" was actually the remains of a mansion built around 1895 by the wealthy industrialist William H. Wesley. Wesley's father, the Reverend John Wesley, arrived in the area in 1885 and filed homestead papers for a home built in 1884. William H. Wesley taught school in Point Washington for a while, and ended up marrying one of his students from the area, Katie Strickland. Wesley then went into business with his father-in-law Simeon Strickland, and they operated a sawmill in Point Washington.

They used the mill to cut yellow heart pine harvested from the area, and shipped it to other locations via Choctawhatchee Bay. Wesley had the mansion built from that same pine, and at 5500 square feet it was the largest home in the area at the time. The business also owned 20 smaller houses and a commissary for the workers at the sawmill. At some point Wesley built a mill of his own, located north of the house on the shore of the bayou. Fire was a common occurrence in the timber industry, especially if you had enemies. According to Wesley's daughter some of those enemies set fire to the sawmill, and it apparently burned down several times. Wood was plentiful, so they rebuilt it, but after the third time they decided not to do it again.

Wesley died in 1947, but his wife Katie continued to live in the home until her death in 1953. The original house as shown circa the 1920s was built in a Victorian style with narrow columns and gingerbread trim on the porches. The roof was topped with a "widow's walk", another enclosed room, and a cupola that permitted observation of waterfront activities around the sawmill. William H. Wesley III wrote that as a boy he was told that when the house was built the upper room permitted a view all the way to the Gulf five miles away. But by the time he lived there the oak trees had grown tall enough to block that view.

The Wesley mansion circa 1920 (Florida State Archives Photographic Collection).

After Mrs. Wesley's death none of the Wesley's nine children were interested in maintaining or living in the home. It was sold in 1955, but the new owner had no desire to renovate it, and the house fell into disrepair. The photo below was taken by a resident of Seagrove Beach during this period, and shows the state of the property circa the early 1960s. This must have been during the period my friends and I saw the property on our Jeep rides. Note the deteriorating railings and steps. Although it's obscured in the photo, I've heard that

The Wesley mansion circa early 1960s after it had been vacant for several years (photo courtesy of Philip and Flip Spann).

the cupola visible in the 1920s photo had collapsed. It's easy to see why we labeled it the 'haunted house'.

Then in 1963, after the house has been sitting vacant for 10 years, Lois Maxon, a wealthy journalist from New York City, purchased the home and about 10.5 acres of property for $12,000. Ms. Maxon was heir to the fortune from the family that owned the Maxon Corporation of Indiana. Although not a household name, Maxon is a leader in industrial combustion equipment such as burners and valves. Ms. Maxon had the house renovated and enlarged, and eventually lived there, finding it the perfect setting for her collection of Louis XVI furniture and antiques that was said to be the second largest in the United States. The giant oak trees and views of the waters of the bay needed no improvement, but she added gardens with roses, azaleas, camellias, and other flowers, and a reflection pool with water lilies and koi fish. The more recent photo after renovation shows it much the same, although some refer to it as antebellum style; the columns are slightly different and the cupola is no longer present on the roof structure. Due to ill health, Ms. Maxon donated the home and gardens to the state of

The mansion after renovation in the 1960s.

Florida in 1968, and it became Eden Gardens State Park.

Incidentally, the little post office I mentioned above started out as one of the small cottages used by the saw mill workers. Helen Strickland, the postmaster at the time, purchased it and moved it to a corner of her property so she could take care of her mother. Before that, the post office had been located in another small mill building that William Wesley moved to the ferry dock in 1936. The Point Washington post office closed around 2007 (Frances Kelley, personal communication, November 25, 2017).

Back in 1895 when Wesley started his mansion, his partner Simeon Strickland built a nearly identical house nearby., It had the same design and floor plan but with a slightly different roof, and without the widow's walk and cupola on top. It's known now as the "Strickland House" and has been used as both a private residence and a historic event venue, although it's not part of the state gardens.

The Strickland House at Point Washington in 2018.

According to a sign at the gardens, traces of the mill used to process the southern yellow pine, including that used to build the two mansions, can still be seen on the Eden grounds. An interesting note from one of the signs says that the restoration of the Wesley house fulfills a local legend claiming that the original design was inspired by an antebellum plantation house where the builder was once given shelter on his way home from the War Between the States. Although somewhat different from most of the attractions in the area since it's not on the beach and doesn't directly represent most of the things people come to the area for, Eden provides an interesting contrast with its idyllic setting and a vision of times past.

Six

Chapter 6. Water Water Everywhere, and a Few Interesting Phenomena

"Water, water everywhere, nor any drop to drink." (Samuel Taylor Coleridge, "The Rime of the Ancient Mariner")

The blue and emerald green waters of the Gulf of Mexico is probably the most famous and recognizable feature of Seagrove and the other beach communities of the Florida Panhandle. And rightly so, as few other locations offer such a striking combination of beautiful water, soft white sand, unique vegetation, and interesting wildlife. However, if you look at any map of the panhandle you'll also notice many other bodies of water, some connected to each other, and others independent. I write here a little about these different bodies of water and what distinguishes one from another. A gulf may be defined as a large coastal indentation, or a large area of a sea or ocean partially enclosed by land. A sea can also be similarly defined, and the distinction is often somewhat blurred. The Caribbean Sea, which is just south and east of the Gulf of Mexico, is about the same size, and is also surrounded by land masses, although not to the extent that the Gulf is. Incidentally, the Gulf of Mexico is considered the largest gulf in the world, with an area of over 600,000 square miles. After the Gulf, the next largest bodies are the bays, such as Choctawhatchee Bay in Walton County, Mobile Bay in Alabama, and St. Andrew Bay near Panama City. A bay is a concave feature in a coastline or a body where the sea cuts into the land. There are many similarities between the definitions of seas, gulfs, and bays. Bays can be relatively open like Apalachee Bay on the Gulf of Mexico, or more enclosed like Choctawhatchee Bay, but they are always connected to a larger body of water like the Gulf. The water in a bay is mostly brackish, a mixture of fresh and salt water, although near the mouth of a river the water can sometimes be considered fresh water. Choctawhatchee Bay has a huge connection to many of the activities in Walton County beach communities like Seagrove Beach. As noted earlier it once formed a barrier to travel to the coast, so ferries and bridges were utilized to cross it, and have been important aspects of daily life for decades. The bay provides sites for activities such as fishing, swimming, and boating. It's also the backdrop for Eden Gardens State Park, Sandestin Resort, and parts of Eglin Air Force Base. The bay is fed by the Choctawhatchee River, and is connected to the Gulf of Mexico through the Destin or East Pass, to Santa Rosa Sound on the west end near Fort Walton, and to the Intracoastal Waterway and West Bay at the east end near Point Washington. I'll discuss the Choctawhatchee River in a moment.

Other fairly large bodies of water that are often found along the shoreline of bays are bayous, which consist of marshy or sluggish wetlands, or a stream or secondary watercourse that is a tributary to another body of water. The water in bayous is often brackish and may be affected by the movement of tides. A map of Choctawhatchee Bay shows Tucker Bayou near Point Washington, Hogtown bayou near Santa Rosa, Horseshoe Bayou near Sandestin Resort, among others.

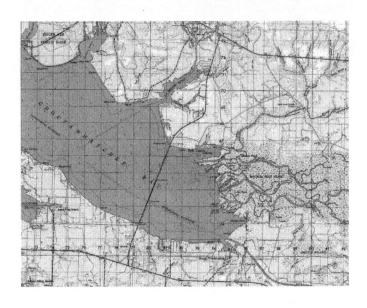

Portion of Choctawhatchee Bay showing some of the many bayous (USGS map).

Like bayous, lakes also consist of a body of stationary water, but, in contrast to bayous, lakes are formed in inland basins, not necessarily in low-lying areas, and contain fresh water. Lakes are often either fed or drained by rivers or streams. There are lots of lakes in Walton County, the most famous being the coastal dune lakes mentioned in Chapter One. Such lakes exist in only a few places in the world. From Fuller Lake near Sandestin at the western end through Powell Lake in Bay County, near the eastern end of CR 30-A, there are a total of 14 dune lakes. According to the nonprofit Choctawhatchee Basin Alliance, coastal dune lakes are bodies of water, typically shallow and irregularly shaped, found in dune ecosystems within two miles of the coast. Usually permanent bodies of water, the lakes are fed mostly by streams, rainfall, and groundwater seepage from uplands and the Gulf. They are close enough to the Gulf that after a heavy rainfall or other inflow, the freshwater of the lake can breach the sand berm and flow into the Gulf. Likewise saltwater from the Gulf can flow into the lake, and because of all these flows their water levels can fluctuate substantially. The lake water is usually very dark, tea colored or even black, due to dissolved organic matter.

Homes have been built around most of them, although part of Western Lake near Grayton Beach, and Deer Lake about two miles east of Seagrove, have been designated state parks and are preserved. Unusual ecosystems have developed in the lakes, and each is unique. Incidentally, the other places that apparently have such lakes are New Zealand, Australia, Madagascar, as well as Oregon and South Carolina.

Map of coastal dune lakes in Walton County (courtesy of the Choctawhatchee Basin Alliance).

The water in all the larger bodies of water comes from rainfall in addition to other sources. In some cases, such as Choctawhatchee Bay, it comes from rivers. A river is a natural stream of water that flows in a channel and has well-defined banks. Rivers and the smaller streams that feed them are fresh water, and get their content from overland runoff, springs, meltwater from snow and ice, and precipitation. Most of the flow into the Bay comes from the Choctawhatchee River, which drains parts of southeastern Alabama and the Florida Panhandle. But at least three other smaller rivers (the Cypress, Indian, and Mitchell Rivers) empty into the east end of the Bay near the Choctawhatchee River. While a river is the largest form of natural stream, a creek usually refers to a small stream, and it has the other characteristics of a river, flowing in a channel with banks. Black Creek is an example of a creek, and it also flows into the Bay.

The bodies of water described above, whether stationary like the bayous or flowing through banks like a river, are all natural. But man-made bodies of water can also be important. The Intracoastal Waterway is a navigable shipping route that extends for about 3,000 miles along the Atlantic Ocean and Gulf of Mexico coasts. The Atlantic portion connects ports from Boston to Key West, and the Gulf Intracoastal Waterway serves ports from Apalachee Bay, Florida, to Brownsville, Texas. Some references list a second section of the Gulf Intracoastal Waterway from Ft. Myers to Tarpon Springs. The Waterway utilizes many natural sounds, bays, lagoons, and rivers, but also depends on man-made canals or channels to connect some of the natural bodies. It was designed to provide a channel 150 feet wide and 12 feet deep, although some sections may not always meet that standard. The portion that connects the east end of the Bay with West Bay near Panama City was completed around 1936. It has been an important resource for shipping throughout its lifetime, and has also been a great resource for recreational boating since it provides a more sheltered route for smaller boats than traveling in the Gulf or Atlantic.

Here are some "short takes" on other characteristics of the Walton County coast:

Why is the sand so white, and why does it squeak when you walk across it?

Anyone visiting Seagrove Beach and surrounding communities will notice that the sand is some of the whitest you can see anywhere, even compared to beaches in other parts of Florida. This is neither an accident nor simply due to bleaching by the sun. According to the Destin Chamber of Commerce website and other references, this sand originated in the Appalachian Mountains around 20,000 years ago at the end of the last ice age. The mountains are composed largely of quartz, and as world temperatures rose and the ice caps melted, rivers carried large volumes of water to the world's oceans. That water carried quartz particles from the Apalachicola Mountains. The Chattahoochee River in Georgia flows from some of those slopes, and the Apalachicola River, formed from the Flint and Chattahoochee Rivers, deposited the particles in the Gulf of Mexico about 100 miles east of Seagrove. Rising sea levels formed the shorelines with this quartz sand, which extends as far west as the Pensacola Pass. It helps that we don't have rivers flowing directly into the Gulf near Walton County beaches, since many rivers carry sediments that can make the water and sand appear darker.

On most days you'll also notice that the sand squeaks when you walk on it. Desert sands have been known to make "booming" sounds since the time of Marco Polo, but those sounds are much louder and deeper and last longer than the squeaks heard at the beach. The two types of sound may be related though, and both require movement of the sand, whether from an avalanche on a dune or the weight of your foot pushing sand out from under it. Several characteristics of the sand grains are necessary for sand to squeak: the grains are usually very similar in size, they must be close to spherical in shape, and their surfaces need to be very smooth. Wave action and currents tend to sort sand particles into groups of similar sizes. The sand on Walton County beaches traveled a great distance from its origin in the Appalachian Mountains, and this movement allowed the surfaces to become highly polished and smooth. An additional factor required for squeaking is that the sand not be too moist. Squeaking is apparently produced by a process called shearing, in which grains slide past each other. Too much moisture prevents this shearing by causing the sand grains to clump together or otherwise altering the frictional characteristics. However, even though we know some of the characteristics and conditions for sand to squeak, the phenomenon is still not completely understood.

Why is there a sand bar, actually two, off the beach?

If you look out at the Gulf from the top of the bluff at Seagrove, one of the most striking features of the water is the bright turquoise color of the sand bar about a hundred yards offshore. Sometimes called the "second sand bar", it is more correctly called a longshore bar or offshore bar, and is formed by wave action. As waves move through an open body of water the motion of the water at the surface is essentially circular. As a wave moves into shallower water and approaches the shore it is influenced by the bottom surface of the body of water. The turbulence of waves excavates a trough in the sand at the bottom. Some of this sand is carried forward by the wave action toward the beach, and some is deposited on the seaward side of the trough, gradually building up a sandbar. Additional sand may be added to the bar by currents, by the backwash from breaking waves, and by sand movement from deeper water. Although the waves are responsible for building the sandbar, they also serve to limit its height by their motion over the top of it. The depth of the top of the sandbar is related to the size of the waves, and true sandbars are normally submerged except at times during a storm, or a period of low water level. Some shorelines have as many as three longshore bars, and the

The two underwater sand bars as seen from the bluff at Seagrove.

number is related to the slope of the bottom and the availability of sediment to form the bars. Incidentally, an offshore strip of sand that rises above the water level is technically called a barrier island. Much of the coast of the Florida Panhandle has barrier islands, but the strip from the east end of Santa Rosa Island at Destin to Panama City does not.

As noted above, the longshore bar is often referred to as the second bar. You'll notice in the photo that you can see a similar looking feature just a few yards offshore. The water in this area is shallow and so it all has the same turquoise color, but there is a shallow trough with a sort of low sandbar seaward of the trough. This is sometimes referred to as the first sand bar, although the bar is more correctly called a ridge, and the shallow trough is referred to as a runnel. This structure also forms as a result of wave action, and sand can be transported toward the beach or away from it depending on the immediate local conditions.

What causes tides, and are there one or two sets of tides per day?

Tides are an unmistakable feature of almost every beach, and Seagrove is no exception. Just set up your umbrella or build your sand castle too close to the water line at low tide and you'll find out in a few hours that the water level rises periodically, often taking sand features and objects with it. Tides are caused by gravity, mostly the gravitational force exerted by the moon as it orbits the earth. The sun's gravity also causes tides, but the effect is only about half that of the moon because the sun is so much farther away. The moon's gravity actually causes the water in the oceans to bulge both on the side facing the moon and on the opposite side (more on that in a minute). So since the earth rotates once every 24 hours, the water at our location will bulge upward once when the moon is overhead, and again when the moon is on the opposite side of the earth from our location, for a total of two tides every 24 hours.

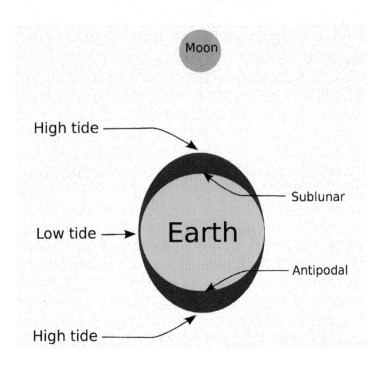

Diagram showing how the moon causes tides on the earth (courtesy of Wikimedia Commons).

The bulge on the side of the earth toward the moon is relatively easy to visualize, because the moon is aligned in that direction and is pulling on the water. But why is there a bulge on the opposite side of the earth too? To explain the other bulge, we need to understand a concept called inertia. Inertia is simply the propensity of any body to maintain its present state of motion, i.e. if the body is moving, it is the tendency to keep moving in the same direction (in a straight line), and with the same speed. Or, if the body is not moving, it is the tendency to stay at rest. To change a body's state of motion requires a force, such as gravity, to act on it. The water in the earth's oceans is essentially dragged around as the earth rotates, and it resists any change in its motion because of its inertia. On the side of the earth facing the moon gravity is strong enough to overcome the water's inertia and pull it toward the moon, causing the bulge on that side. But on the opposite side of the earth, the moon's gravity is weaker than the water's inertia, so the water tries to keep moving in a straight line, and forms a bulge, but this time in the direction opposite the moon. This explanation can also be reframed using the concept of centrifugal force, but must be done carefully since centrifugal force is usually not considered a true force. Incidentally, the moon's pull even causes the earth itself to bulge very slightly. Although this effect is not as readily evident as the effect on the oceans, it is important for such things as Global Positioning System (GPS) measurements and scientific experiments. Many other factors affect tides, such as the varying distance of the moon, the alignment of the sun and moon, the shape of the ocean bottom, winds, and storms. The change in water level from high to low tide in the Gulf of Mexico is small relative to many other oceans, and it is also possible to have one or two complete high-low tide cycles per day in the Gulf.

Why are the sunsets red?

You can't help but notice the beautiful sunsets at beaches like Seagrove, with the fiery red sun and surrounding clouds. Actually the same colors can be seen in most locales, but are often more noticeable from a spot in the mountains or on a beach because of the unobstructed horizon. But why does the sun look red, as opposed to white or yellow as it looks when overhead? The answer is related to another familiar phenomenon in nature, the fact that the daytime sky is blue. If you were to orbit the earth in a spacecraft, above the earth's atmosphere, the sky would appear black in every direction. If the sun was visible it would be a blinding white, but it's light would be visible only if we looked directly at it. But when we look up from the earth's surface we are looking through the earth's atmosphere. As sunlight travels through the atmosphere it is scattered in different directions by the molecules in the atmosphere, so some light reaches our eyes from whatever direction we may look. Also the white light of the sun that is visible when above the atmosphere is actually composed of all the colors of the rainbow, from red to yellow to green to blue to violet. But because of the physics of the scattering process in the earth's atmosphere, blue light is scattered more efficiently than red, so when we look from the earth's surface in a direction other than at the sun, we see mostly this scattered blue light.

Now back to the original question of why sunsets are red. When we look up in a direction away from the sun we see mostly blue light, and that is blue light that has been scattered from the original white light of the sun. If we look up directly at the sun at noon when it's high in the sky, its light is traveling through the earth's atmosphere, but through the shortest path. Some of the blue light is scattered from the light beam, slightly altering the color of the sun, but not enough to notice much. If we look at the sun when it is almost at the horizon, its light has to travel through a longer path in the atmosphere to reach our eyes. So now more of the blue light has been scattered from the light beam, and what is left is mostly red. The longer the light path through the atmosphere, the more blue light is scattered out of the beam, and the redder the remaining light looks.

Why do the moon and the sun appear so much larger when rising or setting?

Since ancient times people have noticed that the moon appears larger when it is near the horizon, and great minds from Aristotle to da Vinci have commented on the phenomenon. This is commonly attributed to atmospheric refraction, the effect where rays of light are bent as they pass through the atmosphere because the density of the air varies with height, temperature, and other factors. But it turns out that refraction does not increase the actual size of the moon's disk, and this can be verified in several ways, such as by taking photos of the moon when it is near the horizon and again when it is overhead. The diameters of the images will be the same. The difference in appearance of the moon when low in the sky vs. high in the sky is truly an illusion, and is often called the "moon illusion". It is a result of what is called the apparent distance theory. Our mind knows that for two objects at different distances to appear to be the same size, the farther object must be larger. So if two objects that are actually the same size are perceived as being at different distances, the object that seems to be farther away will look larger to us. Here's how this applies to the moon. The moon near the horizon appears to us to be farther away, an effect partly dependent on the presence of terrain near the horizon. When viewing the moon our mind automatically takes into account the apparent distance. It then unconsciously applies the fact we saw above, that for two objects that form images of equal size the one that is farther away has to be larger. So the moon near the horizon, that appears to be farther away, MUST be larger, and the illusion is created. The illusion works the same way for the sun, and incidentally also for constellations of stars, like the Big Dipper. Stars, and the constellations we fashion from them, move across the sky as the earth rotates, just like the sun and moon. So you can compare the apparent size of the Big Dipper when it is near the horizon to its size when it is high in the sky and see the same effect.

What causes rainbows, and why don't we always see one after a storm?

Rainbows are one of the most common examples of a spectrum of light, and are formed as light rays interact with raindrops. As a ray enters a raindrop it is refracted, or bent slightly, so it then travels in a slightly different direction. When it reaches the far side of the inside of the drop, it is reflected at a right angle, still inside the drop, traveling at a new angle. Then, as the ray reaches the opposite side of the drop it is refracted (bent) again as it passes into the air. Since the angle at which rays are refracted depends on the color (the wavelength) of the light, and since sunlight (white light) is made up of all the colors, the rays of light leaving the raindrops are traveling in slightly different directions, depending on their colors. This is why the colors are spread out as though diverted by a prism. The reason we don't always see a rainbow and rainbows can be of different length arcs, is because the reflection inside the drops causes the emerging rays to be bunched together at an angle of 42 degrees with a line drawn between the observer and the sun. So the rainbow appears in the direction directly opposite the sun, and if the sun is higher than 42 degrees above the horizon no rainbow will be seen (unless you are on elevated ground or in an airplane). The lower the sun, the higher the arc of the rainbow will appear, and the larger it will be, up to a full semicircle. One last thing - a rainbow is not a physical object actually located at a point in space, but rather an effect caused by directed light rays, similar to your image in a mirror.

You've probably seen photos, or an actual twilight, where after the sun sets the rays emanate from behind a cloud and radiate from the position of the sun. The effect is often surreal and may have a religious feel. These rays, known as crepuscular rays, are also called god rays. The word "crepuscular" comes from the Latin for "twilight" so strictly speaking the effect occurs just after sunset, although a similar phenomenon can be seen during the day when the sun shines through cumulus clouds. This is caused when rays stream through gaps in the clouds or other objects and are scattered by dust particles in the atmosphere. The combination produces the effect of columns of sunlight separated by darker shadowed regions. As hard as it is to see from most photos, the rays are actually traveling parallel to each other, and it is only the phenomenon of perspective that makes them seem to radiate outward from one direction. You get the same effect if you look at a pair of railroad tracks extending off into the distance. The two rails appear to converge and join in the far distance, even though they are parallel. If you could view the rays from above, which has actually been done by NASA from the International Space Station, the parallel nature of the rays would be easier to see.

Crepuscular rays formed when the sun shines through gaps in clouds.

Seven

Chapter 7. The Boston Whaler and the Little Boat House

"A ship in harbor is safe, but that is not what ships are built for."
(John Augustus Shedd)

In the early 1950s a boat designer named Dick Fisher started experimenting with the newly-invented polyurethane foam. He had built sailboats using lightweight balsa wood and realized the new foam might make a good substitute. After consultation with a naval architect friend and much experimentation they eventually came up with a triple-hull design known as a trimaran, made of fiberglass and foam. Although only a little over 13 feet long, the new design was very stable because of the triple hull, and almost impossible to sink even in rough water. The boat was marketed as the Boston Whaler and along with a slightly larger version became very popular. My father was familiar with the design and had friends who used them in in lakes in Alabama such as Lake Jordan and Lake Martin. Since the boat was easily moveable with an optional trailer, he bought one with the idea of using it at Seagrove.

Our Boston Whaler on the trailer at the house.

The Florida Panhandle has many different bodies of water, and we often put the boat in Choctawhatchee Bay using the boat ramps along the causeway on US 331. We usually used the Buick station wagon that transported the family to Seagrove on weekends. These ramps were fairly convenient, although the concrete ones were sometimes very slippery because of the algae growing on the concrete below the water line. The eastern end of Choctawhatchee Bay is a very diverse body of water, with an interesting shoreline and several smaller bays and coves along the shore, The Choctawhatchee and Mitchell Rivers and some small creeks dump into the north shore and provided great starting points for further exploration. At the far eastern end the Intracoastal Waterway, which runs through the Bay, continues east and provides a continuous pathway all the way to the Panama City area and beyond.

Ramps were also available at Western Lake in Grayton Beach and I think we may have found one at Eastern Lake east of Seagrove. We also had a trailer hitch on the Jeep and learned to tow the trailer on the beach. This allowed us to drive down to Eastern Lake and launch the boat into the lake from the sand, or launch it directly into the Gulf. Launching into the surf required experience and calm water conditions, but gave us direct access to the largest body of water. After trying out several of these places my parents decided Choctawhatchee Bay was a good compromise - much bigger than any of the lakes, with more room to explore, but not as dependent on weather conditions as the Gulf. Although the boat ramps along US 331 were fairly convenient, they figured it would be nice not to have to hook up the trailer and go through the processing of launching and landing the boat every time we wanted to go out. So they looked around and found a small housing development called Daugettes. First developed in the late 1950s, it was on the south shore toward the east end of the Bay, and only about five miles from Seagrove. The important thing for us was that the subdivision included a small channel, maybe half a mile long, that ended in a basin about 300 feet square.

Plat map of Daugettes Subdivision on Choctawhatchee Bay. The boat channel and basin are in the center and center right of the map (Walton County, Florida).

A few of the lots had homes, some with piers. There was a two-slip boathouse in the basin, and my parents rented one of the slips. This way the boat was sheltered from sun, rain, and any rough water in the Bay, but always ready when we wanted to use it. The whole family often went out, and we took a picnic lunch and cruised to the north side of the Bay or to the east end and into the bayou or Intracoastal Waterway. Fishing could be a little crowded with four people on board, but when we did fish we usually tried near the mouths of the rivers, in the bayou at the east end, or around the pilings toward the north side. Redfish, speckled trout, mullet, and catfish are some of the species found in the Bay. By the way, those pilings are apparently a source of wonder for many people driving by or boating in the Bay. There seem to be hundreds of them, but I've never read anything definitive on the origin or use. The fact that many have shaped metal reflectors attached to the top makes me think they are, or were, used for military training with the aircraft at Eglin Air Force Base north of the Bay. The array of pilings with reflectors may have provided a radar signature or a visual target for training flights.

Recent photo of the basin at the end of the channel from the bay, where the little boathouse was located.

Recent photo of the channel leading to Choctawhatchee Bay from the boat basin. At the far end is a turn to the right where we beached the Whaler, tipped it up, and scraped the barnacles off the hull.

Although having a slip offered many advantages, having the boat in the water all the time definitely had its drawbacks. Since Choctawhatchee Bay was fed by rivers but connected to the Gulf, the water was brackish, or a mixture of saltwater and fresh water. This meant that certain salt water marine life could live there, including barnacles. Barnacles are crustaceans and thus related to lobsters and crabs, but unlike those cousins, barnacles are immobile. They attach themselves permanently to a hard surface, such as a piling or the hull of a boat. I'm not sure we ever suspected these would exist in the Bay, but after keeping the boat in the boathouse for a few months we began to notice a change in performance. As more and more barnacles grew on the hull, the hull surface became less smooth, and the additional water resistance after a while made it impossible to get the boat up into planing position, even at full throttle. We didn't look forward to dealing with this problem, and if we had tried to put the boat on the trailer the rough hull would have made it hard on both our backs and the trailer. So we hatched a plan that involved the little canal. Most of the canal had vegetation right up to the waterline, but at the 90 degree bend in the canal on the plat map above, there was a little sand beach on the inside of the bend. So one day my father and I gathered some putty knives and other scrapers and set out to clean the hull. We drove the boat out to the bend and beached it. Then after unloading the gas tanks and removing the motor, we got next to one side and tipped it up on its opposite side. Since the boat was resting in sand we didn't have to worry about scratching or damaging the hull, and by pushing some extra sand against the hull in various places it was stable while tipped up. It took a few hours of scraping but we got the intruders off the hull, put the motor back on, loaded her up and were back in business. I don't remember exactly when or why we stopped renting the boathouse, but it served us well, and then the boat went back on the trailer and back to the house. I'll discuss the Boston Whaler again in the chapter on remembering Cube and Babe McGee.

Eight

Chapter 8. Exploring the Dunes and Digging for Pottery

"You can see a lot just by observing."   *(attributed to Yogi Berra)*

The high bluff that helps make Seagrove Beach unique extends to the east almost to Eastern Lake and to Western Lake in the other direction. The land behind the bluff is mostly flat and this area was developed first. But in the area between the lakes and the Gulf, the wind over the years has formed dunes of varying heights, extending inland a few hundred yards. About a mile beyond Eastern Lake is Deer Lake, and another mile brings you to Camp Creek Lake. The areas in front of and between these lakes are also occupied primarily by dunes. Back in the 1960s there were fewer roads and although you could sometimes park along CR 30-A and on some unpaved roads leading into the woods, access to these areas was not always easy. But with our Jeep we could pack a picnic lunch, drive down to the beach and up to Eastern Lake, and work our way up through the dunes between the lakes. At that time there were no restrictions on driving on the beach or in the dunes, unlike today where only a few vehicles are allowed and must have a permit. So we would

Some of the dunes near Deer Lake, where we had picnics. The dune walkover is part of Deer Lake State Park, and was added later (photo courtesy of Alice Forrester).

often look for a spot to eat lunch, and then walk around in the dunes. The dunes were always dynamic and fascinating, with areas of pure white sand, others covered with patchy grass and all sorts of windblown or waterborne debris, and still others dotted with thick bush and scrub oak trees. Some of the trees appeared to be decades old and indicated that the dune in that spot had been anchored and stable for a long time. But in other areas with little or no vegetation the dunes could change rapidly. Wind constantly changed the shape, and rain and windblown debris could erode the surface. Low areas often showed signs of having been flooded during recent storms, which provided another means of changing the surface.

When walking or driving in the dunes we soon began to notice interesting objects. An unusual piece of driftwood might catch our eye, or a shell. Shell casings from ammunition were also not unusual. I don't remember exactly how or when we first noticed a piece of pottery, and whether we were aware that such things might be found there. But eventually we found some pieces, often called potsherds, sometimes lying on the surface and sometimes partially buried. Quite often these were single pieces, but occasionally we would find a cluster of pieces, apparently originating from the same pot. Eventually, after lots of walking and looking, and lots of false alarms, we learned how to spot pieces, and how to increase our odds of finding something. For example, looking up at the broad slope of the side of a dune while walking below it allowed us to see a lot of area at a glance. Having a slope that was relatively free of vegetation and debris also improved our chances, since it was hard to spot small pieces if they were mixed in with small plants, twigs, leaves, or anything else of similar colors. Although most pottery was much darker than the white sand, if a piece was covered with even a thin layer of sand we would never see it. So we made a point of going after storms, which we knew would have reshaped the dunes with their wind, rain, and sometimes with surface flow of water. Changes in the top layer of sand, even if slight, increased our chances of finding something. The bigger the storm, the more anxious we were to get out in the dunes and see what might have been newly uncovered.

As discussed in Chapter One, Native Americans of several tribes inhabited south Walton County. Many potsherds have been found at sites such as the Mack Bayou mound near Choctawhatchee Bay, but I haven't found sources stating explicitly how close any tribes lived to the beach. The largest pot we found, of which about one third to one half of the pot has been pieced together, would have an overall diameter of about 10" and be about 7" tall, with a thickness of about 1/4". The color ranges from tan to dark brown, but it's not clear whether this was part of the design or the result of weathering of the material. It has regular indentations all around the necked-in portion of the rim.

The largest pot we found, which would have an overall size of about 10" in diameter by 7" tall.

The smaller pot section appears to have had a much shallower overall shape. The section shown below has an overall size of about 6" long by 4" tall, and the full pot might have been about 8" diameter by about 4-1/2" tall. The color is close to black, and it is thicker than the large pot, with a thickness of about 1/2". The surface is very rough and grains are constantly sloughing off, as though this pot was made of a material different from the large one, or processed differently, or perhaps it was exposed to much different environmental conditions during its lifetime. No surface markings are visible, although any that were there would likely have been affected by the material coming off the surface.

This smaller pot is noticeably shallower than the large one, with an estimated overall diameter of about 8" and a height of about 4-1/2".

The mosaic of pieces shows that the colors can range from brown or black to tan and noticeably reddish. The pieces range from 1" long by 1" wide to 3" long by 3" wide. Although neither of the pot sections above have many surface markings, we found some pieces that were covered with interesting patterns. The piece shown below, which is about 3-1/2" long by 2" wide, has an interesting pattern that consists of areas delineated by a perimeter line and filled with an array of dots, with the lines and dots indented into the surface. The color of this piece is ruddy-tan to brown.

This mosaic of individual pieces shows the range of colors, surface textures, and patterns we found in the dunes of South Walton.

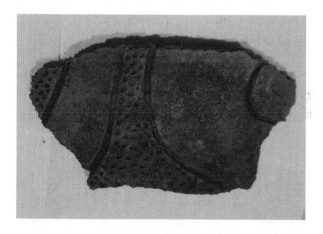

An individual piece from the mosaic above that shows a dense surface pattern of lines and dots.

Although most of the pieces we found were in the dunes around and between Eastern Lake and Deer Lake, and which form some of the larger dune areas along the immediate coastline, that doesn't mean there wasn't pottery to be found in other areas. Also we tended to have a lot of our picnics and do much of our hiking in that area, so we were probably more likely to find things there. Recall that in the 1960s before the beach road was called CR 30-A and before it extended west to Grayton, the road ended just west of Seagrove Beach, about where Cyprus St. forms the western boundary of the early Seagrove. And although Grove St. and Forest St. to the north also ended, some sand trails extended further west, into the area that is now Seaside. It was in dunes along one of these trails that I found my favorite piece of pottery. As the photo below shows, this piece, or possible pair from the same pot, shows a hexagonal or octagonal rim instead of the more common round rim. It is of an almost pure black color and has markings that include straight and curved parallel lines as well as small indentations like dots. Also it is the only piece we found that has a handle, in the form of a ring attached to the rim. The piece is about 3-1/2" long by 2" wide, and from the shape it looks like the full pot might have been possibly about 6" in diameter. It's difficult to estimate the height since the piece is from the rim area only, but I would guess possibly 4" to 6".

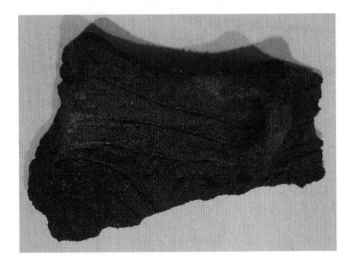

An individual piece having a polygonal rim, varied markings, and a ring-like handle.

An expert on Florida artifacts who examined some of these photos estimated the pieces were made sometime between 1000-1600 CE, and are known as Mississippian forms (Neill J. Wallis, personal communication, November 30, 2017). The Mississippian culture was probably an ancestor to most if not all the tribes that lived in this region, although the expert said it was not possible from the photos to identify the specific people who made these. To narrow down the date range when these were made, a scientist can sometimes use radiocarbon dating, also known as carbon-14 dating. This radioactive-decay-based method of dating organic materials works because most plants and animals contain tiny amounts of the radioactive isotope carbon-14. This form of carbon is usually created when cosmic rays strike nitrogen-14 atoms in the earth's upper atmosphere and transform them into carbon-14. The newly-created carbon-14 atoms oxidize to become carbon dioxide and are later taken up by plants on the earth's surface. If an animal eats one of the plants it gets into the act too, because it absorbs some of the radioactive carbon-14 that was in the plant. This dating method works because when the plant or animal dies, the radioactive carbon begins to decay at a known rate, so scientists can determine the age of the organism by measuring the amount of carbon-14 remaining in a sample. You may note that pottery is usually made from some form of clay, which is not considered organic, but pottery often has traces of soot stuck to its surface. This soot, a by-product of burning some organic fuel such as wood, is organic, and the age of the pottery can often be determined by scraping off some of the soot and analyzing it using radiocarbon dating. This method could probably narrow down the date range of these pieces, but it can be expensive, and at this point will be a possible project for the future.

nine

Chapter 9. Plants You're Likely to See, and a Few You May Not Want to See

"To such an extent does nature delight and abound in variety that among her trees there is not one plant to be found which is exactly like another; and not only among the plants, but among the boughs, the leaves and the fruits, you will not find one which is exactly similar to another."   *(Leonardo da Vinci).*

With mild temperatures and lots of rain the Florida Panhandle has an abundance of vegetation. One of the first plants you'll notice, long before you get to Seagrove Beach, is the pine trees, a ga-zillion of them. In some areas it seems like they're growing next to every roadway and filling every forest. They are native to the area and grow well in Florida's fairly poor soil. Much of what you see is slash pine, although there are also longleaf pine and other varieties. Slash and longleaf pine are both members of a group referred to as southern yellow pine, which is widely used in construction. The value of timber for construction was one of the reasons this part of Florida was developed. Another big user of pine trees is the paper industry. In the early 20th century, Alfred Dupont of the Dupont family sent his brother-in-law Edward Ball to purchase timberland in northwest Florida, eventually amassing about one million acres and becoming the largest landowner in the state. He originally bought the land assuming the land boom in south Florida would spread to the northern part, but that didn't happen as soon as anticipated. However, one of the land purchases included the town of Port St. Joe, as well as a sawmill and railroad associated with the town, and Dupont envisioned a paper mill to resurrect the town and the surrounding area. After his death in 1935 the St. Joe Paper Company was formed, and for 60 years it followed Dupont's vision, growing trees and turning them into paper. In the 1960s we saw many tracts of timberland with small concrete markers that read "SJPC", which we eventually learned indicated they were owned by the St. Joe Paper Company. And although the pine trees on the land were used in papermaking for another 30 years, the papermaking industry was not considered environmentally friendly. Also by the late 1990s a land boom had hit the panhandle, and because of this and other factors the company decided to concentrate on developing the land for residential and commercial purposes rather than harvesting the timber. It changed its name to the St. Joe Company and developed Watersound among other communities on CR 30-A.

Once you get into Seagrove Beach you'll notice its famous scrub oak trees. Scrub oak is a name given to multiple species in the area, including the myrtle oak and the sand live oak. These smaller cousins of the live oak have leaves that are often smaller and more curved, with the edges rolled over. Although they may grow fairly upright in some places, in Seagrove Beach they are often gnarled and the trunks may grow horizontally for some distance. Live oaks may become much larger, and form the beautiful canopy at Eden Gardens State Park in Point Washington.

Sand live oaks, usually called "scrub oaks", at our first house.

Alongside the oaks you'll often find beautiful flowering magnolia trees. Although not thought of as a tree you'd see close to the ocean and salt spray, some homes in Seagrove have magnolias growing almost to the edge of the bluff. A tree that is usually associated with beach areas is the palm, and Seagrove has its share of those. The most common palm is the cabbage palm, or sabal palmetto, which is the state tree of Florida. There is also a grove of cypress trees between Seagrove Beach and Eastern Lake, a few hundred yards inland from the Gulf, off Cypress Street in the neighborhood of Cassine Gardens. The grove stands in a low, swampy area, surrounded by the pine forest on slightly higher ground. The trees grow on hummocks, small raised mounds above the surrounding ground, the same type of mounds referred to in Chapter One, although on a different scale. I think because of the location and setting that

Cypress swamp located north of CR 30-A just east of Seagrove Beach.

these are Atlantic white cedar or false-cypress, a species that resembles the popular arborvitae sometimes used for hedges. Cypress trees are in the conifer family, like pines, although most cypress have a slightly different leaf that is flattened and scale-like. Like other conifers, cypress trees have both female and male cones. The female cones, also known as seed cones, are usually woody and larger than their male counterparts. The male, or pollen, cones are smaller and often wither and die after the pollen is released to fertilize the seed cones. Another member of the cypress family common in the area is juniper, also known as red cedar or southern red cedar. It is smaller than the Atlantic white cedar but also very aromatic, and is found on the dunes and in open and sparsely wooded areas.

There are many more species of trees and other plants in the area. Varieties of holly such as Yaupon and American holly are also found in the woods, the marshes, and the dunes. Their leaves are often evergreen and their fruits or berries are usually red. The word Yaupon comes from the language of the Catawba Native American people, and some sources report that both the leaves and berries were used to cause vomiting. Saw palmetto, a member of the palm family, is easily recognizable by its fanlike leaf blades. Wax myrtle is common, and wax from the berries can actually be used to make candles.

Pittosporum grows well in this beach environment, and is often grown as a hedge. The striking Spanish bayonet, a species of yucca, can be found both in wooded areas and out in the open. It is related to some southwestern plants like the Joshua tree, and has evolved thick waxy leaves to retain water. The plant is sometimes grown as an ornamental, with spectacular white flowers, as shown in the photo.

Spanish bayonet in bloom on the bluff.

If you explore the bluff and walk the dunes you'll see some of these same species, but they have to be hardy and resistant to the wind and salt spray to survive. You're more likely to see a series of hardy vines in this region. You'll find several species of morning glory, such as fiddle-leaf, arrow-leaf, and coastal morning glory. And a variety known as beach morning glory or railroad vine is perhaps the hardiest. It gets its name from the long straight runners it sends out, some of which may extend over 30 feet. At least one species of sunflower is also common, the cucumber-leaved or beach sunflower. A common grass is seaside panicum, also known as bitter panicum or running beachgrass. Another is known as gulf bluestem or the related maritime bluestem. But far and away the best-known grass or plant on the dunes and beach is sea oats. In addition to having beautiful seed heads resembling oats, it serves an important purpose in accumulating sand and aiding in the development and stabilization of dunes. Unlike many plants that would be injured or killed by being covered with sand, sea oats actually thrive in such conditions, as the underground stems send out new roots when covered. With a name and appearance a lot like the breakfast cereal, maybe it shouldn't come as a surprise that the seeds may be cooked and eaten, and are apparently very tasty. Although sea oats may not be an endangered species, due to their popularity and the tendency for visitors to take some with them, it is illegal to pick them in some places,

Sea oats in the Florida Panhandle (Florida
State Archives Photographic Collection).

There are also some plants that grow a little differently from all these others. The first is Spanish moss, and it is most evident hanging from the branches of the giant live oak trees at Point Washington's Eden Gardens State Park, When the wind is calm, its appearance helps to create the serene atmosphere. But when a storm is brewing the swinging of the Spanish moss reflects the agitation in the air. Even though this spaghetti-like gray plant looks somewhat like moss, it is actually a relative of the pineapple. It's an epiphyte, which means it has no connection to the soil and grows on another plant, but it gets no food or water from the host plant, and so is not a parasite. Since it must derive all its water and nutrients from the surrounding air, it has adapted to do just that. Both the stems and the threadlike, filament-shaped leaves have tiny scales that trap both water and dust particles, the latter providing some of the nutrients the plant needs. By the way, take a closer look at the branches in the photo of the live oak. Do you see what look like ferns growing on top of some of the branches? They are called resurrection ferns, another epiphyte like the Spanish moss. These ferns have a long, winding root system that extends into folds in the bark, harvesting rainwater that collects there. Nutrients come from dust and may also leech out of the tree itself. The name resurrection fern may derive from a couple of characteristics of these companions. The resurrection fern has developed an amazing resistance to drought, able to lose up to 97% of its water content without dying, as compared to most plants, which begin to die after losing as little as 10% of their water content. It is able to do this because of an adaptation that allows its fronds to curl inward, reducing

Spanish moss growing on a live oak in Point Washington.

water loss by minimizing the amount of exposed surface area. Some researchers have estimated that this fern can live up to 100 years in its dry state, only to return to life in a matter of hours after a rain or an increase in humidity! And there's more; it is also recorded in literature from indigenous people of the region that members of the Seminole and Miccosukee tribes used the fern in baths to treat insanity, and made a mixture containing this and another type of fern to treat other health conditions.

Another plant that grows a bit differently from the others is the water lily, visible on Deer Lake and several other coastal dune lakes. Although the leaves are usually seen floating on the water surface, the plants are rooted in the soil beneath the lake and the leaves emanate from a horizontal underground stem called a rhizome. Some have leaves that are deep purple on the underside, and they produce beautiful flowers, on top of the leaves, one reason they have been a favorite subject of artists for centuries. While we're on the subject of the dune lakes, some of the most abundant plants you'll see around Eastern Lake, Western Lake, and Deer Lake are common arrowhead or duck potato, black or needle rush torpedograss, and sawgrass.

We've mentioned many types of plants, some of which grow in the water, and the Gulf of Mexico hosts additional species, such as seaweed. It turns out seaweed isn't actually a plant, because it's formed of various types of algae, and algae are technically neither plants nor animals. Algae range all the way from single-celled organisms floating freely, to colonies or filaments, to complex plant-like structures. But unlike higher plants, algae do not have true roots, stems, and leaves. One of the common seaweeds on the Gulf coast is sargassum weed or gulfweed. Sargassum is a floating brown macroalgae that was first discovered in the Atlantic Ocean in an area that became known as the Sargasso Sea. The name may have come from the Greek word for grape, because the structure has small air bladders that resemble grapes. However, some sources say the word sargasso came from the Portuguese word for a plant called the rock rose. While floating in the open ocean sargassum colonies support a community of organisms such as fish that use the colony as a source of both food and protection from predators. Because the floating colonies are subject to the force of the wind, large quantities are regularly deposited on Gulf beaches, sometimes affecting beach use because of the mass of material and the odor. Another alga species that affects Florida coasts is *Karenia brevis*, and in high concentrations during an algal bloom it causes the phenomenon known as the Florida red tide. These tiny organisms turn the water a grayish or reddish color, and contain a neurotoxin that affects both fish and humans. When ingested, the toxins can paralyze the gills of the fish, causing the fish to die. When ingested by shellfish such as oysters and shrimp, the toxins can sicken humans since they are not destroyed when the shellfish are cooked. When present in the air the toxins may also cause human respiratory problems. Although Spanish explorers reported these toxic red tides as far back as the 1500s, scientists still don't have a good understanding of what causes them.

Of course not all plants are 'friendly' and nice to look at. Some plants you may not want to run into, but probably will, include poison ivy, sandbur, and thorny vines such as greenbrier. Although my family never had problems with poison ivy, it can be very poisonous on contact to some people. Poison ivy can be found in many places including woods, fencerows, swamps, marshes, and even the dunes. In contrast to poison ivy, sandbur and greenbrier are two unfriendly plants I've had a lot of experience with. Sandbur looks almost like short lawn grasses and can be found anywhere from the dunes to – you guessed it – your lawn. The problem with this 'grass' is that it hides little burs that have spines and can get lodged on socks and pants legs and be a real pain to remove. I used to run into these when mowing the lawn and when walking in the dunes along the beach. If you encounter them, you'll probably remember the occasion. Greenbrier is another unwelcome plant. There are several varieties of this thorny vine, and I used to run into them on the slope of the bluff. My least favorite has leaves with large side lobes at the top, and I used to call it 'horsehead' vine. These can surprise you and cut up arms and legs, depending on which areas of skin you have exposed. Incidentally, an extract from the roots of some related species is used to make the drink sasaparilla, or sarsaparilla, a type of root beer. Finally, there's prickly pear cactus. You might not expect to find a desert plant near the seashore, but despite the abundance of surrounding water, the almost incessant wind of many shore areas tends to dry out plants. For this reason, many plants well adapted to life near the beach have developed ways to preserve water, such as the thick outer skin of a cactus, thick leathery leaves, and sometimes water storage tissues in the plant. The prickly pear cactus fits this description, and can be found anywhere from sparse woods to the dunes. Needless to say if you don't notice one of these and brush against it, you could get some painful spines in the skin. Although not very friendly if you don't know how to handle it, the prickly pear is actually quite useful, and parts of it have been used to treat everything from asthma to ulcers. It's also edible, with juice from the red fruits used to make cakes and juice. Cooked pads are a healthy alternative to green beans.

Finally, see a note in Chapter 22 on Deer Lake about another 'plant' that's actually not a plant, even though it's usually called a moss.

Ten

Chapter 10. Surfing Cube's Canal, and the 'Discovery' of Western Lake

"Mistakes are the portals of discovery (paraphrased)."
(James Joyce, "Ulysses")

After the initial plat of Seagrove and the development of the land along the bluff and on the north side of CR 30-A, C.H. McGee, Sr. made more additions extending further east along the beach and north into the forest. The roads had names like Grove Street and Forest Street in one direction, and Dogwood, Hickory, and Live Oak in the other. This was fitting, since the land was densely wooded. Another feature that predated the development was a little stream or waterway running east to west, north of all these streets. According to topographic maps of the area the stream started well east of CR 395, ran underneath the road, and continued west to Western Lake, which extends to Grayton Beach and has an intermittent connection to the Gulf. After C.H. McGee, Sr.'s passing, Cube and Mrs. McGee, Sr. created a new addition to Seagrove which included an east-west street running along that little waterway, labeled as a canal, with a single row of lots between the street and the water. The street was named

Canal Street and the addition was called "Seagrove Shores". The intent was to provide sites where homes could be built along this 'canal' and to promote it as a usable body of water. I've been told that Cube had the canal dredged to try to maintain a useable width and depth, and we referred to it as 'Cube's canal'. The addition was platted in 1958, and after my parents bought our house we didn't notice very many, if any, homes on Canal Street.

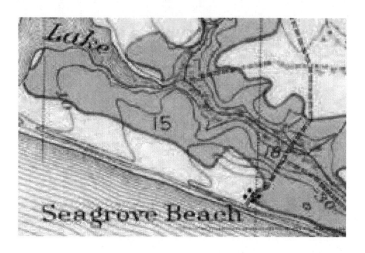

USGS topographical map from 1939 showing the stream that we later referred to as "Cube's canal".

By about 1964 we had our Jeep at the house and had used the Boston Whaler in several of the local waterways, as discussed in Chapter Seven. The canal hadn't been used much and many parts were badly overgrown with marsh grasses and shrub. One day Cube and my father got the idea to put the Whaler in the canal and make a run down the length of it. I'm not sure why Cube didn't want to use his boat, but suspect there were several reasons. Our Whaler was slightly shorter and didn't require as much depth to operate. We had a smaller 18hp outboard motor compared to Cube's, which I think might have been a 40hp, so ours was lighter and easier to handle. Also Cube's boat was a standard V-hull runabout, while the Whaler was a very stable triple hull design. He probably suspected we would be spending a lot of time leaning over the side dealing with the vegetation and other obstacles, so the stable hull would be an advantage.

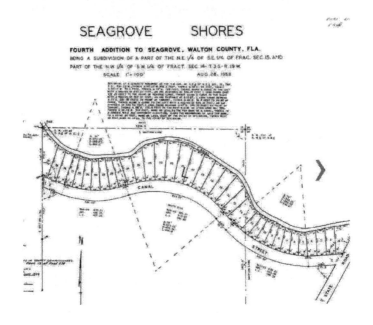

Plat map of Seagrove Shores subdivision. The little creek, or canal, is shown running along the top boundary of each of the lots (Walton County, Florida).

I don't remember exactly where we launched the boat, but it had to have been west of CR 395 because the passage under the road was a culvert, and the boat wouldn't have fit through it. Since we had Jeeps and a trailer I suspect we launched just west of the road from one of the vacant lots. Once the boat was in the water the real fun started. Since the canal was only a few feet deep at best, we had to creep along constantly watching for the bottom. We ran most of the time with the outboard motor partially tilted up so it wouldn't drag the bottom and pick up a lot of the long grass. Regardless of that precaution, the propeller constantly became fouled with the grass, forcing us to stop, tilt the motor completely out of the water, and clean off the propeller by hand. But nobody said it would be easy, and we pretty well knew to expect this when we started. After a couple of hours we made it to about the end of the long row of lots where Canal

Street ended, and then turned around for the return trip. It was a lot of work, but the scenery was nice and we had a sense of satisfaction when it was completed. Although there was nothing along the canal in those days and we didn't follow it all the way to the lake, later developments have made good use of the canal. For example, the Watercolor subdivision has a couple of bridges over it with a road and a walking path, and I've seen people kayaking in the canal.

Another nice spot to launch the Whaler from the trailer was at Grayton Beach. Western Lake forms much of the eastern boundary of Grayton, and there was a concrete boat ramp at the end of one of the roads. The part of the lake that borders Grayton was a nice size, large enough to cruise fast and to explore a couple of legs that extended northward along the east side of Grayton and into the woods. There was a little channel along the eastern side of the lake as viewed from Grayton, but as far as we knew it was just a feeder and wouldn't be very navigable, like Cube's canal out of Seagrove. In the early- to mid-1960s CR 30-A ended just west of Seagrove Beach, Seaside hadn't been founded, and Grayton Beach State Park wasn't there. To get from Seagrove Beach to Grayton you had to drive north from Seagrove on CR 395 to US Highway 98, go three miles west to CR 283, and then go about two miles south to Grayton. So even though we had some

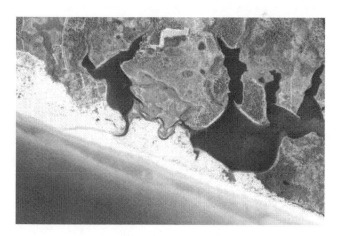

1949 aerial photo showing the tiny channel connecting the portion of Western Lake near Grayton Beach to the left to the larger portion of the lake to the right (USGS).

maps of the area, the features on the two miles of land between Grayton and Seagrove weren't all that clear because no roads extended into the area.

One day while cruising Western Lake my father and I found ourselves at the mouth of the little channel and decided to see how far along it we could go. But even with the same techniques we had used in Cube's canal, such as tilting the motor partially out of the water, the channel soon became so shallow that we just couldn't make any progress using the motor. So we turned off the motor and tilted it up completely out of the water. I took off my shoes, grabbed a rope, hopped out into the water, and towed the boat with my father in it. This was possible because of the small depth and size of the Whaler. We couldn't see around the bends in the channel up ahead, and when we started we didn't know whether the channel would connect to anything before the depth petered out to nothing. But after a little while we were rewarded when a huge lake opened up in front of us. This is why I claim we 'discovered' the much larger part of Western Lake, the part not visible from Grayton or any of the roads. We had a really fun day of exploring in the large part of the lake, after which I towed us back through the channel to the smaller part of the lake, and we motored back to the boat ramp.

A few years later CR 30-A was extended from Seagrove, across the large part of Western Lake, to Grayton. Grayton Beach State Park was opened in 1967, complete with a picnic area, camping, and a boat ramp directly into the large part of the lake. So now it's much easier to get to that part of the lake, but current visitors don't have quite the pristine landscape we had in the 1960s, and certainly not the sense of awe we had when we 'discovered' Western Lake.

Picturesque line of slash pine trees near Western Lake.

Eleven

Chapter 11. Some Unexpected Creatures

"It is quite possible that an animal has spoken to me and that I didn't catch the remark because I wasn't paying attention."   (E.B. White, "Charlotte's Web")

With it's mild climate, forests, and many bodies of both fresh and salt water, the Florida Panhandle is naturally host to a myriad of animals in addition to its abundant plant life. And the Gulf of Mexico is home to a wide variety of fish, ranging from mackerel to tuna, mullet to swordfish. Red Snapper and Marlin are popular catches for charter boat fishing, along with Grouper, Cobia, and Tuna. Surf fishing is also popular, with Pompano, Redfish, and Cobia some of the desirable catches. Yes, there are sharks, and stingrays as well, although they seldom interact with humans. Sharks live in all the oceans on earth and so it shouldn't be surprising that they inhabit the Gulf of Mexico. Rays are a closely related species or sister group to sharks, and many types live in the Gulf. Stingrays are the best known, thanks in part to publicity and word-of-mouth communication whenever someone is stung, and it's common to see them in the Gulf. After the death of 'crocodile hunter' Steve Irwin in 2006 from a stingray attack the reputation of stingrays as deadly killers grew even more widespread. But that was apparently a truly freak occurrence and is not representative of the animal's normal behavior. I remember once when I was attending a show at the Gulfarium in Fort Walton Beach, the lecturer made a point of talking about stingrays and the misconceptions surrounding them. He explained in detail that it's very rare for them to attack, that the geometry of their stinger is not conducive to attacking humans, and that you essentially have to corner them and then jam a body part into them in order to get stung. They're still scary because of their appearance and reputation, but not a true threat to humans at the beach. Another type of ray, the manta ray, is a relative of the stingray although somewhat different. Manta rays don't have a long tail and a stinger like stingrays, and rather than eating small crustaceans and fish, they are what are known as filter feeders. They swallow large quantities of water and strain small organisms like plankton from the water. When piloting a boat from deep water into the shore my father and I once saw a manta ray that was perhaps six feet across. The creature was lightning fast and pretty exciting, but not a threat. Whales also inhabit the Gulf, but mostly in deep water, so you're not likely to see one. They are not fish but mammals. Once in the 1960s we found one on the beach in Seagrove, probably washed ashore after it died. It was about six to seven feet long, and my guess it that it was a sperm whale, the largest of the toothed whales.

Sea turtles are also fairly common in the Gulf and are classified as threatened or endangered. Surprisingly, they are air-breathing reptiles, but very well suited to life in the sea. Although born on land, after their first crawl to the ocean, sea turtles never return to the land except the females to lay their eggs. Since the eggs are laid on the beach it should be possible to see a sea turtle on land, although I've never seen one on the beach. I did see a very large one out in the Gulf a few years ago. I was sitting in the house casually watching the ocean and noticed several times what appeared to be a large bird way out in the water. It's common to see birds diving for fish or sometimes floating on the water, so at first I didn't think too much of it. But I was surprised at the large wingspan and the fact that it seemed to be threshing around in the water. After a while I got out my binoculars to take a closer look and only then realized I was seeing a bird at all, but rather the flippers of a large sea turtle. I think it must have been a leatherback because of the overall size and the size of the flippers. I watched it for several hours and later went out in a small raft when it got closer to shore. I never got really close to it but from a distance it seemed to be the size of a Volkswagen Beetle.

A loggerhead turtle laying her eggs on the beach (Florida State Archives Photographic Collection).

Another frequent dweller in the warm Gulf waters is the jellyfish, also known as a medusa because its family of tentacles resembles the ring of snakes worn by the mythological monster. Jellyfish are not true fish and in fact are one of a group of animals called zoo-plankton, where plankton refers to a marine organism that cannot swim against wind-driven currents. Jellyfish propel themselves by rhythmically contracting their bell-shaped bodies, and feed on everything from plankton to small fish and other jellyfish. They use their tentacles to capture prey and to defend against predators. The ctenophore, or comb jelly, is closely related to the jellyfish, and is so named because it is ringed with rows of tiny hairs that resemble combs. In contrast to the pulsations of true jellyfish, comb jellies propel themselves by moving these tiny hairs, and most do not have tentacles. Probably the strangest animal resembling jellyfish is the Portuguese Man of War, which is not a true jellyfish, or a fish, or in fact even a single animal. This strange creature is actually a floating colony of organisms called polyps, working together to survive. A gas-filled bladder on top serves as a float for the rest of the colony, and it actually has a 'sail' on the bladder to provide propulsion via the wind. Transparent tentacles trail behind the float, and are specialized either for capturing food or for providing defense.

A Portuguese Man of War on the beach at Seagrove.

The toxic venom of the Portuguese Man of War and some jellyfish is delivered by explosive cells called nematocysts that contain a coiled hollow thread with a sort of dart on the end. This remarkable capsule uses a special protein that stretches and releases energy to essentially fire the dart into the target animal, where it injects the venom and can cause painful lesions in humans. With an acceleration of up to a million times the force of gravity (g's), it is said to be the fastest object in nature. Pretty efficient for a floating colony with no 'brain'!

Crabs are, of course, ubiquitous at the Gulf. One of the most common types is the sand or ghost crab, which are often seen right on the white sand, and make their burrows in the sand. Blue crabs are usually found in shallow water and form an important food source. Although we only tried to catch sand crabs at night for fun, and always let them go, crabbing for blue crabs is also popular. One of our neighbors often set a crab trap in the shallow water in front of his house and had a steady haul of blue crabs available for eating. Mole crabs, sometimes called 'sand fleas', are usually seen right at the water line, and burrow into the sand as each wave recedes. They are often used as bait when surf fishing. Another animal referred to as a crab that exists in the Gulf is the horseshoe crab, but these are not true crabs. Although horseshoe crabs resemble crustaceans, animals with an external skeleton or exoskeleton, they are actually more closely related to arachnids, a biological class that includes spiders. Females lay their eggs in a hole in the sand, but they are not often seen on the shore. But once, back in the 1960s, we were at Seagrove and found dozens if not hundreds of horseshoe crabs on the beach. I don't know what caused them to beach at that particular time, but we never again saw them on the beach in such large numbers.

In the shallow water near shore, or out at the second sandbar, it's possible to find several types of snails, starfish, and sand dollars. Sand dollars are a type of sea urchin called a keyhole urchin. You might also see other types of urchins, most of which are much thicker. The keyhole variety, or sand dollars, evolved their flattened profile so they can quickly escape under the sand. Their slot-shaped holes interrupt the flow of water over them to help prevent waves from lifting and propelling them toward the shore. Although Walton County beaches generally don't have a lot of shells, you will normally see a least a few small ones near the water's edge. The small bi-valves often found near the water's edge with the two shells connected are a type of clam. It's also common to find cockles and scallops.

Before we leave the sand I'll mention another animal that makes burrows along with the crabs, an animal that's almost too small and elusive to see, but too important to ignore. It's the Choctawhatchee Beach Mouse, and it's considered endangered and critically imperiled. These small brown and white colored mice reach a length of about five inches and come out of their burrows at night to forage for seeds, fruit, and insects. They are threatened by development along the beaches, which causes degradation and destruction of the dunes. Other threats include human traffic, hurricanes, and predation by other local animals such as foxes and raccoons.

Many birds can be seen along the Gulf coast, with gulls, terns, herons, and pelicans being some of the most common. It's almost impossible to go to the beach and not see many of these. Pelicans are known for flying in a "V" formation, also known as "en echelon", which requires less energy for the birds behind the leader. You'll often see them flying like this over the beach or the bluff. Herons are more often seen in quiet, still areas of water, and can also be seen around docks.

A gull on the beach at Seagrove. Gulls and terns are similar in appearance and I think this is a Herring gull.

With all the forests in Walton County and the mild weather land animals are abundant, and we often see evidence of snakes, possums, racoons, and skunks. We often took our dogs, a German shepherd and a poodle, to Seagrove with us, and since the shepherd stayed in the yard, there was always a chance he would have a run-in with a wild animal that strayed onto the property. This never caused a problem until the time he tangled with a skunk. He was none the worse for wear, but smelled pretty bad. So we resorted to a 'folk' remedy we had heard about...tomato juice. We bathed him in several cans of it, scrubbed him briskly, and then took him down to the beach for a swim in the surf. He wasn't thrilled about all the scrubbing, but that plus the action of the salt water and his thrashing around did a pretty good job, and after a while he was back to normal. I imagine he recognized skunks after that and stayed clear, since it never happened again. Actually some of the animals I've mentioned, like snakes, can be found on the land or in the water. Most of the snakes we saw on land were lying in the road after being struck by a car. But we also used to see them in the water when boating, which was unnerving if you happened to be moving slowly or were moored and they swam up under the boat. One group we read about but never saw were alligators, and that suited us fine. I've read enough stories about human interactions that I don't need to see them unexpectedly.

In August of 1970 we had possibly our most unusual visitor, one who was comfortable on both the land and in the trees – a gibbon. I was away at college when my father captured several great photos, and only recently found out the true story of this little guy. After checking several books and the Florida Fish & Wildlife Conservation Commission trying to figure out where he could have come from, I learned that he belonged to the neighbor's son from Birmingham. It seems that when Elton Stephens' son Jim was visiting Sumatra around 1970 someone gave him an infant gibbon as a gift.

The gibbon sitting pensively outside our screened porch.

Jim named him after the country of origin and promptly brought him home to Alabama and raised him with the family's Fox Terrier and Irish Setter pups. I guess that explains why they look so comfortable together in the photo.

Here's Sumatra swinging on the branch of a scrub oak tree.

And out for a romp with his "siblings".

We didn't have a fence around the front yard toward the beach, and I guess it wouldn't have made much of a difference. Jim told me gibbons are the world's greatest limb swingers, and it looks like it from the other photo. I think these prove that any species, even from the far corners of the earth, can enjoy life in Seagrove Beach!

Twelve

Chapter 12. A Bigger Boat and New Waterways

"Then he looked behind him and saw that no land was visible. That makes no difference, he thought. I can always come in on the glow from Havana." *(Ernest Hemingway "The Old Man and the Sea")*

The Boston Whaler served us well. We used it in lakes, the eastern end of Choctawhatchee Bay, Cube's canal, Western Lake, rivers ending in Choctawhatchee Bay, and the Gulf. We kept it on a trailer at the house part of the time, and at the little boathouse on the Bay at another time. Although it was one of the most versatile boats made, my father had designs on a larger boat that had more room and was more suitable for open water. He still wanted something that could be moved on a trailer if necessary, and preferably something that could be stored out of the water. There were lots of marinas and dealers in the Destin and Fort Walton areas, and he looked at a number of boat designs, which the dealers were more than happy to demonstrate in the Bay and the Gulf. It seemed like a good time to compare boating options. Manufacturers had plenty of experience with wood, aluminum, and fiberglass for hull materials, and fiberglass designs were available in both single skin (one layer) and sandwich (two layers of fiberglass with foam in between) designs. The hull could have either a single V shape, or multiple V's, like a catamaran with two hulls, or a trimaran with three hulls. There were plenty of options for powering a boat, too. Inboard motors were used in most larger boats, but outboards from Johnson, Evinrude, and Mercury were popular on smaller boats. Our Boston Whaler used an 18-hp Johnson outboard motor. Another design called an inboard-outboard motor, or stern drive, combined the motor location in the hull from the inboard motor, and the drive unit outside the hull from the outboard motor. My father finally settled on a fiberglass sandwich multiple hull design, similar to the Boston Whaler, but with two stern drives for propulsion. Both the boat and the motors were made by Outboard Marine Corporation (OMC), the company that made Johnson and Evinrude outboard motors. The inboard-outboard design offered more power than similar outboard motors, and my father liked the dual motors since we would be using the boat in larger parts of Choctawhatchee Bay and in the Gulf. The photo below shows a similar hull design but with a single outboard motor. Since this boat was much heavier than the Boston

A tri-hull boat similar to our OMC, but with an outboard motor instead of dual stern drives (Florida State Archives Photographic Collection).

Whaler, my father didn't think it was a good idea to trailer it and try launching at multiple sites. Instead he selected a marina that offered inside storage in Fort Walton, at the west end of the Bay, using a warehouse-type design with boats stacked three-high on racks and moved to the water with large fork-lifts with extended-length forks. It was a pretty good compromise in terms of convenience. We couldn't get storage like that near Seagrove, but Fort Walton was an easy drive (at least in those days), the marina was right on the Bay, and we didn't have to spend time hooking up the trailer, filling portable gas tanks, launching, etc.

We cruised all over the west end of the Bay, where bayous and coves led to the small towns of Shalimar, Valparaiso, and Niceville. We would also cruise further up the length of the Bay to the east, or to the pass at Destin and out into the Gulf. Choctawhatchee Bay ends at Fort Walton, but Okaloosa Island, which forms the southern border of the Bay and separates it from the Gulf, extends westward becoming Santa Rosa Island. The narrow body of water west of the Bay and north of the island is called Santa Rosa Sound, and it extends west to Mary Esther and on to Navarre Beach and Pensacola. This was a fun waterway to boat in since it passed through

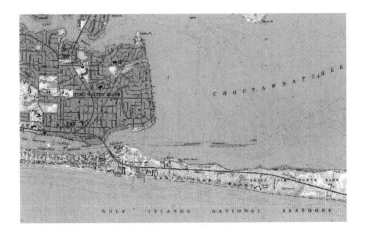

Map showing the west end of Choctawhatchee Bay and Santa Rosa Sound. The marina was located adjacent to the bridge across the sound (USGS).

a variety of terrain and was fairly narrow, allowing high speeds because of the generally smooth water. The Bay itself and Santa Rosa

Sound are all part of the same Intracoastal Waterway that extends to the east end of the Bay and beyond, where we used to cruise in the Boston Whaler.

My father and I would sometimes head west from the marina into Santa Rosa Sound, enjoying views of homes, dunes, and other watercraft. And we occasionally saw other interesting items, too. Most of the area north of Choctawhatchee Bay and Santa Rosa Sound is part of Eglin Air Force Base, and that is the source of a lot of air traffic. Eglin is the largest Air Force base in the country, extending over several hundred square miles on land, and an additional several thousand square miles in the Gulf. Built in 1935, it is home to many units of several branches of the military and has served as a test site for numerous manned and unmanned aircraft and missiles. Since many training missions are flown out over the Gulf, lots of aircraft fly over Santa Rosa Sound. I remember one day we were heading east back to Fort Walton after cruising down toward Pensacola when we saw something bobbing low in the water. We went over for a closer look and found what looked like some sort of unexploded bomb. It could have been a dummy device used in training missions, but we weren't going to get close enough to find out whether or not it was live. My father let me have a nice, but safe, look at it, and then said in a serious voice "We will not mention this to your mother when we get home, understood?" On another occasion we were cruising west on Santa Rosa Sound and a police or Coast Guard boat stopped us. The officer asked where we were headed and what our plans were. When my father replied that we were just pleasure cruising the officer responded that a missile was being launched over that stretch of the sound at a certain time that afternoon, and that it would be closed to all traffic during that period. The officer didn't say what type of missile was being tested that day, but Eglin had a long history with missiles. It was the first to test the Air Force's JB-2 flying bomb, an early cruise missile that was in fact a copy of the V-1 developed by Germany in World War II. And recent news accounts tell of Tomahawk cruise missile testing near Eglin. Anyway, we arranged our plans to make sure we would be back past that stretch of the waterway by the appointed hour.

A JB-2 Flying Bomb taking off from Eglin Air Force Base in 1947 (Florida State Archives Photographic Collection).

Our OMC boat saw split duty, sometimes with the whole family, and sometimes with my father and me. We did some fishing with it in the Bay, although not as much as we did with the Boston Whaler. We also occasionally fished on charter boats from the Destin fleet, such as Olin Marler's charter boat, and had some great catches both in the Bay and in the Gulf. My parents also enjoyed surf fishing from the beach in front of our house, using large spinning tackle. After my sister and I were in college my parents sometimes went on overnight deep water charters from Panama City fishing for sailfish, and they got some beauties.

My father with a sailfish caught off the coast of Panama City circa 1970.

Thirteen

Chapter 13. Some Historical Hurricanes That Affected South Walton County

"There are some things you learn best in calm, and some in storm."
(Willa Cather, "The Song Of the Lark")

Hurricanes are a fact of life for both the Atlantic and Gulf coasts of the United States, and beach communities have always had to face them. And while each storm does some form of damage and leaves some mark, certain storms end up being memorable. Whether because of the shear strength of the storm, the time of season, the number of people and structures in the path, or some other combination of factors, certain storms will never be forgotten. I'd like to review a few of the storms I've read about, so they form a context for direct treatment of more recent storms I'll talk about later.

Although it is well outside the range of dates I will cover in this chapter, I would be remiss not to include a description of a hurricane in northwest Florida that changed the course of history. In August of 1559 the Spanish explorer and general Don Tristan de Luna y Arellano sailed to a spot near present-day Pensacola, bringing about 1500 settlers and soldiers. The intent was to establish a port settlement, and then travel inland through Georgia and the Appalachian

Mountains to the Atlantic coast to establish a Spanish colony in what is now South Carolina. After several private attempts to establish colonies had failed over several decades, King Phillip II provided funding for this substantial effort. The settlers spent several weeks clearing the forest and starting the construction of housing, and offloaded most of the supplies from the ships, except for the main stores of food. Luna sent some of the soldiers inland to find native people who could help them in their planned journey, and prepared some of the ships for travel back to Spain to report. But on September 19, without warning, a hurricane that had already devastated Puerto Rico hit Pensacola Bay and destroyed most of the ships and nearly all of the food supplies. For the next two years the settlers struggled to survive, but despite several relief fleets from New Spain, eventually all the inhabitants were relocated, and what might have become the oldest continuous settlement in the United States was abandoned. That title instead belongs to St. Augustine, founded in 1565, and thus the hurricane of 1559 truly changed the course of history.

The first hurricane I found mentioned over and over as being particularly devastating was the so-called Great Miami Hurricane of 1926. The storm was first spotted in the Atlantic on September 11 and reached the equivalent of a Category 4 storm by September 16. It caused major damage in the Bahamas and other islands and made landfall near Miami on September 18. It produced the highest sustained winds ever recorded in the United States up to that time and damaged or destroyed most of downtown Miami. After crossing southern Florida the storm traversed the Gulf and made additional landfalls in Alabama and Mississippi on September 20 and 21. Pensacola endured hurricane force winds for an extended period and the storm tide destroyed most of the waterfront structures on Pensacola Bay. Grayton Beach was hit hard and, according to an early resident, the beach was swept off into the high dunes and there were no signs of any lake outlets all the way to Destin. An early house in Grayton, purportedly built by its namesake Charles T. Gray and probably also used as a hotel, is often referred to as the Washaway, possibly based on what the storm almost did to it.

The Washaway in Grayton, which was severely damaged in the Hurricane of 1926.

The storm may have contributed to the formation of the present inflow at Choctawhatchee Bay known as the East Pass, although most sources I have read attribute that change to storm surge in 1928. There is more on this in the section below on 1928. On a national level, the storm is considered to have ended the economic boom in South Florida at the time and may have contributed to the start of the Great Depression.

The most famous storm of 1928, the San Felipe-Okeechobee Hurricane, did not reach northwest Florida, although at least two hurricanes did strike the panhandle in August. I've included them in this list because several references including a report from the United States Army Corps of Engineers indicate that storm surge that year from a violent storm formed the present East Pass of Choctawhatchee Bay. Other references indicate that local residents opened the current

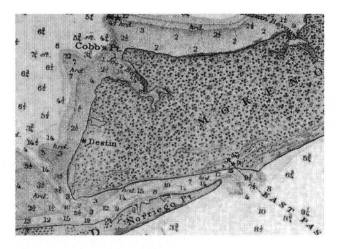

Map of Choctawhatchee Bay and Destin in 1910, showing the old location of the East Pass (courtesy of Florida Center for Instructional Technology, University of South Florida.

pass in 1929 when particularly heavy flooding in the Choctawhatchee River raised the level of the Bay about five feet. Whatever the exact sequence, events of that period resulted in the formation of the East Pass channel at its current location. It had formerly been located about one and a half miles to the east of the present location, and flow was intermittent. Before the formation of the present outflow the Bay was

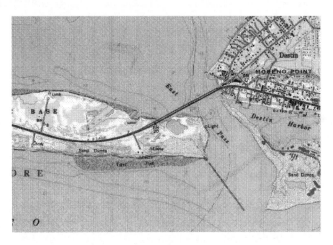

Map of Choctawhatchee Bay in 2000, showing current location of the East Pass. The old location was 1.5 miles to the east, to the right of the label "Destin Harbor" (USGS).

apparently much less salty, and the incursion of salt water caused major changes in plant life, which led to major changes in animal populations, too.

The hurricane season of 1936 was not particularly damaging for the panhandle or for Florida as a whole. I include the hurricane that hit near Fort Walton Beach on July 31 because an account from a Grayton Beach resident indicated that it severely damaged the Grayton Hotel, tearing off porches and causing other damage.

Although additional hurricanes hit the Florida Panhandle during the following decades, the next really severe storm to affect South Walton County was Hurricane Eloise in 1975. Eloise started forming around September 13th in the Atlantic and developed into a hurricane by the 16th. Although weakening for a while into a tropical storm, it regained hurricane status in the Gulf of Mexico. On September 22nd and 23rd it strengthened rapidly before making landfall as a major storm east of Fort Walton Beach on the 23rd. The National Hurricane Center considers storms of categories 3, 4, and 5 on the Saffir-Simpson wind scale to be major storms, and Eloise made landfall as a Category 3 storm, the first major storm to hit the area in the twentieth century. The Great Hurricane of 1926 was more powerful when it made landfall in Miami, but was apparently weaker when it made landfall in the panhandle. And Hurricane Camille in 1969 was more powerful, but did not make landfall close to Walton County. Eloise, on the other hand, was essentially a direct hit, and the winds and storm surge caused extensive damage. According to the National Weather Service, 85-90% of the buildings between Fort Walton Beach and Panama City on the south side of US Highway 98 were damaged or destroyed. Some accounts report that, in Panama City Beach, motels, restaurants, cottages, convenience stores, and other businesses were strewn across the highway and there was a tangle of power lines and poles. Wind and water inundated the first floor of some businesses, and pushed debris out of doors and windows. That debris was pushed inland for hundreds of yards, soaked with saltwater and covered with seaweed. Many motels on the south side of US 98 were built on concrete slabs rather than deep pilings, so when storm surge washed the sand out from under the slabs, the foundations crumbled and the buildings went with them. Several other amusement businesses suffered damage, and some ended up closing for good. One named the Skyride offered gondola rides and views from a height of 100 feet. It was severely damaged by the storm and never reopened.

We'll mention others in a later chapter covering landmarks that no longer exist.

The Round Towner Hotel in Panama City Beach after Hurricane Eloise (Florida State Archives Photographic Collection).

Beach stairs, also known as dune walkovers, were of course very vulnerable, and many were destroyed by the storm. In the Grayton area, beaches and dunes were severely eroded and many bridge approaches were washed away. Many families in Seagrove and Grayton have stories of the damage they saw and suffered, and some accounts say it took 20 years for the beaches to fully recover from the effects of Eloise. According to photos I have, Eloise did a lot of damage to the screened porch of our house, next to a glassed-in porch or 'Florida room'. A later storm actually blew the screened porch away entirely, but my mother never liked that porch, and she was happy to see it gone. Ironically the storm may have actually helped some people and communities. In some cases the destruction of an old school of attractions paved the way for new ones. While much of Panama City Beach was devastated, Destin used the opportunity to advertise the fact that it was still open and welcoming tourists.

Although Hurricane Frederic in 1979 had slightly stronger winds and lower pressure than Eloise, it made landfall in Alabama around Mobile, and did not cause major damage in the Destin to Panama City area.

fourteen

Chapter 14. How (Not) to Stay Warm on Top of a Sand Dune

"The best laid schemes of mice and men go often askew." (Robert Burns, "To a Mouse")

One of the consequences of Seagrove's being far from any big cities is that the sky is often very dark and clear at night. Everyone quickly notices how many stars there are, how dark the background sky is, how bright the Milky Way can be, how close the moon appears, and so on. I mentioned earlier that when I was in school my parents encouraged my sister and me to bring friends with us when we went down to the beach for a weekend or a vacation, and I invited my friend Larry several times. Larry and I had met at high school in Montgomery through a science club, and quickly learned that we shared an interest in both science and music. Our paths had never crossed before because he had just moved to Montgomery when his father, a career Army officer, was transferred in to teach at the military graduate school at Maxwell Air Force Base. The main science interest Larry and I shared was astronomy, so when we got to the beach we spent time almost every night star gazing from the bluff in front of our house. Although we often used binoculars and a small telescope, at a site as good as Seagrove even looking at objects with the unaided eye can be fun and rewarding. For thousands of years man has been consciously or unconsciously grouping stars together, noticing patterns, drawing mythological figures, and forming what are called constellations. Almost everyone has heard of the Big Dipper and the Little Dipper, Scorpio the scorpion, and Orion the mighty hunter. We tried to find and learn the shapes of all the constellations that were visible, including all the fainter and more obscure ones. We learned the names of all the bright stars, knew where Jupiter, Saturn, and the other bright planets were on a given night, when the moon would rise and set, and on and on. Another celestial phenomenon most people have seen is meteors, but these are much harder to see in an urban setting because they're usually not very bright. Seagrove provided an excellent spot for observing these as well.

The bluff was a great spot to observe from, but one time we decided to try to find an even better spot, ideally one with no lights from surrounding houses or the road. Although the bluff gave us an ocean horizon to the south, we thought about finding a place where we could see well in all directions. Back in the mid to late 1960s there was much less development around the dune lakes to the east, Eastern Lake, Deer Lake, and Camp Creek Lake, and with the Jeep we had full access to the beach. The beach itself was not high like the bluff at Seagrove, so we scouted around during the day for a high dune around one of the lakes, and tried to find one that didn't have much vegetation on the peak. As I recall, we settled on one between Deer Lake and Camp Creek Lake, far from the lights of Seagrove Beach, where we could see all around with no lights in any direction. This was intended to be an all-night affair, so we gathered our warm clothes and camping gear and loaded the Jeep. We didn't want a tent since we would be star gazing but we definitely needed sleeping bags and blankets. Also since we wanted to be as high as possible and to be comfortable we figured having cots would be better than being directly on the sand, so we packed a couple of cots, too.

It was definitely winter, probably December or March, and even at Seagrove it can get pretty cold, especially in the early morning hours and if the wind is blowing. We had the clothing and the sleeping

Recent photo of dunes between Deer Lake and Camp Creek Lake in the area we used for star gazing (photo courtesy of Alice Forrester).

bags, but we hadn't allowed for the fact that being on the top of a dune not only gave us a better view, but also put us at the full mercy of the wind. The cots only made the problem worse since we were above the highest point of the dune, and our bodies lost heat in all directions. We had great fun for a while, but eventually the cold and wind had soaked all the warmth out of us and we were concentrating more on staying warm than on what we were seeing. So first we tried getting out of the sleeping bags and moving around to generate more body heat. We thought about moving the cots off the top of the dune into a low hollow to reduce the wind, but didn't want to give up the best view. Finally we decided we needed to build a fire to warm ourselves up. We selected a low point, maybe a few hundred feet from the cots, gathered driftwood and brush, and pretty soon had a fire going. Even with the wind whipping around we were able to warm our hands and bodies without getting too much smoke, so it definitely improved things. But then we got a bit creative, and had the bright idea that if we held the sleeping bags over the fire, we could fill them with warm air, carry them back up to the cots, and start

Painting by Mary Bruns of sand dunes representative of ones near Deer Lake (photo courtesy of Maunsel White).

out observing again nice and warm. Or so the plan went. We got the fire stoked just right, picked up the sleeping bags, and held them up as high as we could to clear the fire but get the benefit of the warm air. Now since Larry's father was in the military, he had loaned Larry a regulation Army issue mummy sleeping bag with the best down insulation, optimum shape, etc., very good and very expensive.

The plan went well at first as we felt the hot air filling the sleeping bags, but just when we were about ready to close up the bags and head for the cots, Larry screamed "Oh s---!" He had looked down and noticed his sleeping bag was on fire and down feathers were blowing around in the hot air above the fire. He immediately slung it onto the sand and began covering it with sand to put the fire out. That didn't take long, but a quick inspection afterwards showed that he had burned several holes in the outer lining of the bag. Larry's father was a very nice man and absolutely fair, but he could also be stern at times, and I remember Larry moaning that he didn't even want to think about going home and facing his father after that. Anyway, at that point there wasn't much we could do. At least the combination of the fire and the excitement had warmed up our bodies for a while, so we went back to the cots and observed until morning. Then we packed up the Jeep, drove back to Seagrove, and slept in for most of the day. I don't remember exactly how Larry's father took the news about the sleeping bag, but Larry's still around, so I guess it all worked out.

Fifteen

Chapter 15. The Making of a Movie at Eden

"Be not deceived; God is not mocked: for whatsoever a man soweth, that shall he also reap." (King James Bible,   Galatians 6:7)

Almost everyone has heard of the 1998 movie "Truman Show" starring Jim Carrey. Many people have seen it, and many also know that it was filmed in the town of Seaside near Seagrove Beach. But did you know that a movie was also shot at Eden Gardens State Park? As noted in an earlier chapter, the house and land that became Eden has a long and interesting history dating back to around the time when Point Washington was founded. A lot has been written about the mansion and gardens, and the website of the state park has information. But something that is not as well known is that Eden was once the setting for a movie, and it provided a fitting backdrop for the unusual characters in the story; but more on that in a moment.

Another movie that almost everyone has heard of is Alfred Hitchcock's classic thriller "The Birds". Filmed in 1963, the movie tells the story of a small California town that is mysteriously attacked by flocks of aggressive birds. It stars Rod Taylor and Tippi Hedren, in her screen debut. The movie was based on the novella by the famous British author Daphne Du Maurier. Although "The Birds" was not very popular when first published in 1952 in a collection of stories called *The Apple Tree*, Du Maurier had earlier written the best-seller *Rebecca*, which sold several million copies. Some of her other works also remain quite popular, and you may have seen the movie made from her story "My Cousin Rachel" in 2017. But back to "The Birds". In Du Maurier's story a disabled farmer tries to protect his family from hordes of birds that attack their cottage in Cornwall, England. Hitchcock's adaptation is set in a small coastal California town. He proceeds slowly, taking time to introduce the characters and their relationships before any action begins.

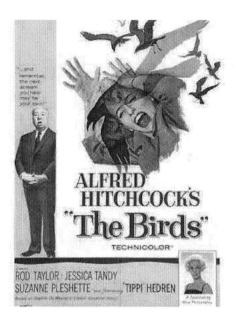

Poster from Alfred Hitchcock's movie "The Birds" (photo courtesy of Wikimedia Commons).

The gradual escalation of attacks by the birds heightens the suspense. Despite skepticism by some, the attacks intensify and eventually the entire area is under attack, leading the main characters to flee, with their fate undisclosed at the end. The movie was critically acclaimed and won several awards. It was even selected for preservation in the National Film Registry of the United States Library of Congress.

So how is this connected to Eden? Well, about 10 years later, in 1972, the film "Frogs" was released. It also depicts a family victimized by animals, but instead of birds, this time it is snakes, birds, lizards, and other reptiles. Falling in the eco-horror category, the film is centered around a wealthy family living in a mansion on an island. Since the story is set in the South and the island is surrounded by swamp, Eden was the perfect setting. It stars Ray Milland as the patriarch, along with Sam Elliott, Joan Van Ark, and Adam Rourke.

As the story begins a wildlife photographer (Elliott) is canoeing through a swamp taking photographs of local plants and other wildlife. The photos are intended for a story on pollution in an ecology magazine, and the photographer suspects the signs of pollution he notices are caused by the use of pesticides on the plantation. After a member of the upper-class Crockett family (Rourke) accidentally tips over the photographer's canoe, family members take him back to the mansion, where he meets the rest of the family including the wheelchair-bound patriarch (Milland). Milland's character is the domineering type and he is intent on celebrating both an upcoming holiday and his birthday at the house. Several family members complain about the growing number of frogs on the property, and are bothered by the noise they make. Milland dislikes most animals, which he sees as pests, and sends a man to spray pesticide in the area to get rid of them. However, the photographer later finds the man dead, killed by snakes.

Ray Milland and Sam Elliott were the protagonists in the movie "Frogs", filmed at Eden Gardens State Park and the surrounding area (inset photos courtesy of Wikimedia Commons).

A gradual series of similar encounters go either unnoticed or unheeded by the inhabitants, until several in the party decide they want to leave. They depart in a boat driven by Milland's son and make it to the other shore. But after the boat drifts away from the dock, the son is killed by a snake, so he can't return for the others. The photographer and the rest of the family depart the island soon after in a canoe, leaving only Milland at the house, since he refuses to join them. As the night progresses he watches as hundreds of frogs enter the house. Amid the rising tension he collapses and apparently dies, leaving the frogs to take over. The house was used in many interior and exterior scenes, and was where Milland's character died at the end.

I was away at college by that time, but my parents heard about the production and drove over from Seagrove Beach on several occasions to watch the filming. Although stars like Sam Elliott and Joan Van Ark were not yet that well established, Ray Milland was a household name from movies like "Dial M For Murder" and "Love Story". Although the Wesley mansion and Eden State Gardens grounds got lots of exposure, apparently the filming took a toll on the location. According to one newspaper account, it was a good thing the antiques and other furnishings were put into storage during the filming, because the movie-making operation caused some damage. There was also speculation that not all the animals used in the filming were retrieved, and that some escaped into the surrounding area. The Panama City area was able to capitalize on the filming since the cast and crew stayed at hotels there and interacted with the public. The premier was held at the Florida Theater in Panama City, complete with Hollywood-style spotlights crisscrossing the sky. And the animals for the production were supplied by the local attraction Snake-A-Torium, which may also have been used as the site for some of the outdoor scenes.

Cast members from the movie "Frogs" signing autographs in Panama City (Florida State Archives Photographic Collection).

Naturally, since my parents were so fond of the area and had watched the effort go into the film, they were anxious to see how it turned out. They went to see it in Montgomery when it was released in March of 1972, but unfortunately my mother told me it wasn't exactly a classic in theaters. It has since built up a cult following, and is apparently considered a fairly good "bad movie". And regardless of film reviews, any visit to the Wesley mansion at Eden Gardens State Park is bound to be memorable.

Sixteen

Chapter 16. A Bad Night in Panama City Beach

"Experience is simply the name we give our mistakes."
(Oscar Wilde)

Up to now I've related mainly stories of family activities, good wholesome fun, etc. Those experiences have helped define the paradise Seagrove Beach has always been for my family and me. However, lest you think I'm just all about picnics, swimming on the beach, and boating with the family, I will tell at least one more worldly story. When I left for college in New England I couldn't get to Seagrove nearly as often as I had, although I still looked forward to going there every summer when I returned home to stay with my parents in Montgomery. One week, around 1969 or 1970, a high school friend from Montgomery and I decided to go down for a few days to swim, drive around, walk the beach, and so forth. My friend went to the University of Alabama and was an excellent student and very hard worker, but he also had a lifestyle that included a lot more drinking than mine did. One evening we decided to have a few drinks at the house and then drive in to Panama City Beach to check out a well-known place we had heard about, known as the "Hang Out". You may think that the fact that we were going to drink and then drive was not the best order in which to do those activities, but we were college age, and our brains, as they say, were not fully developed yet. So we sat down at the kitchen counter/bar at home and had some simple drinks like bourbon and Coke. And we had several of them, which was more than I usually had. Then, even though I was feeling pretty loaded, my friend insisted that since we were just sitting there, the alcohol couldn't possibly be circulating in our bloodstreams yet. So to help accelerate the circulation, he suggested we go out in front of the house on the road (CR 30-A) and do a few sprints. I didn't really see how that was needed, but remembered that this was a guy who drank a lot more often than I did. So I thought 'oh well' and went along with it. You might wonder how we would even think about running down the middle of the road. But I remember the road was empty, so that

The Long Beach Hang Out near Panama City Beach circa the 1960s (Florida State Archives Photographic Collection).

gives you an idea of how much less developed the area was in the late 1960s. By the time I was done with the sprints I was feeling very intoxicated, but we were determined to go, so we got in the car and drove (with me driving, naturally) our not-yet-fully-developed brains into Panama City.

The Hang Out consisted of a long open-air building with separate food outlets and other amusements. The building had a sound system, and the large wood floor could be used either for dancing, skating, or just partying. The place was very well known and had been around since the late 1930s or early 1940s when it opened at the Long Beach Resort. But I had never been there since my family spent more time in Destin and Fort Walton than in Panama City Beach. I'm not sure how many people actually danced, since, as the name suggested, the main idea was to meet people and socialize. We arrived safely, parked the car, and started walking over to check out the scene, but we didn't even make it inside before two plain clothes policemen started questioning us. I must have been the giveaway; as I said we got there fine, but I'm sure they had lots of experience spotting kids who had been drinking. Whether my answers were correct or not, I don't remember, but I know my speech was slurred enough to give me away. Since they were onto us so quickly they may have seen me get out of the car, and probably could have justified writing me up for driving under the influence, but they didn't. It seemed that they wanted to send a message we would remember, but not cost us a fortune or jeopardize my license. So they gave me a ticket for something like disorderly conduct, which got their point across. On the other hand, they weren't about to let me drive home in that condition, so they took us to the police station and gave us a chance to call someone for a ride home. My parents were at home in Montgomery, so I think I called either Cube McGee or a man in Seagrove my parents had known for a long time and who had done repairs at the house for them. Anyway whomever it was that I managed to reach, he showed up an hour later to drive us. Mercifully, I don't think he asked us anything about the circumstances the whole way back to Seagrove. The hour-long ride home seemed to take forever, and I'm sure he knew we were suffering enough. We got home, went to bed, and slept very late the next morning. Of course, my car was still in Panama City, so we had to get someone to give us a ride back to Panama City to pick it up, and the whole time we re-lived the experience of the night before. The rest of the trip was somewhat muted because of this incident, but we made it back to Montgomery okay and eventually I returned to school. We had to fill out some more paperwork and pay a fine, but it was all done by mail.

I believe there were some important take-aways from that ordeal, other than of course that you shouldn't do your driving after your drinking. First of all, boys will be boys, and unfortunately we have to learn most lessons by making the mistakes ourselves. Finally, there are enough patient, kind adults in our lives (in addition to our parents) that most kids make it to adulthood safely like we did. And hopefully we live to repay the favors to our own and our friends' children. Thank goodness for kind adults.

Seventeen

Chapter 17. Some Landmarks That Are No Longer Around, and Some That Are

"A rock pile ceases to be a rock pile the moment a single man contemplates it, bearing within him the image of a cathedral."
(Antoine de Saint-Exupéry, "The Little Prince")

As in any community, attractions, landmarks, and historical places come and go, and sometimes the story surrounding the closing of a place is as interesting as that of its opening. Here in roughly chronological order, according to the construction or opening date, are some of the many landmarks and attractions that have come, and sometimes gone, in and around Seagrove Beach. This listing is by no means exhaustive, and is admittedly colored by my experiences and first-hand knowledge. Also it is limited roughly to the stretch of beach from Fort Walton Beach to the west to Panama City to the east.

An early **Grayton Hotel** may have evolved from a house reportedly built in Grayton Beach around the 1890s by the town's namesake, Major Charles T. Gray. Known as the Washaway, the building was later owned by Walton Land & Timber Company and was used to house its workers making turpentine.

In 1922, W.H. Butler built a new Grayton Hotel on a different site, after he had bought or traded for most of the land in Grayton a few years earlier. The Hurricane of 1936 tore off the porches and caused other damage, and after Butler died later that year, his wife gave up the hotel business. Accounts indicate that their son Van R. Butler, Sr. used wood salvaged from the hotel to build the Grayton Store, known as Butler General, in 1937. He may have also used some of the salvaged wood to build four cottages, two of which were destroyed by Hurricane Eloise in 1975.

Between 1895-97 William H. Wesley, owner of a sawmill in Point Washington, built the Victorian-style **Wesley mansion** there for his family. They lived in the house until the early 1950s, after which it fell into disrepair. This is the home featured in Chapter Five as the "haunted house", and it was later bought by Miss Lois Maxon in 1963 and restored and enlarged. See the later entry on Eden Gardens State Park for the continuation of the story of this beautiful house, and Chapters Five and Fifteen for photos of the mansion.

About the same time William Wesley built his family's home, his business partner and father-in-law Simeon Strickland built an almost identical home nearby. Known as the **Strickland house**, it has undergone some architectural changes and served as an event venue, but is now a private residence visible near Eden Gardens in Point Washington. There is a photo in Chapter Five.

Like Grayton Beach, Seagrove also had an early hotel. The old **Seagrove Hotel** was built sometime around 1920, and appears on an original plat for Seagrove drawn by the Seagrove Company in 1922 and shown in Chapter Four. It was located at what is now the intersection of CR 395 and CR 30-A, an intersection that is still the center of Seagrove Beach. Mazie Ward Rossell ran it in the mid-1930s with her father J.J. Ward. And it was apparently there when C.H. McGee, Sr. bought the development from J.R. Moody and the Seagrove Company in 1949. Although it's not there now, I haven't been able to find the date it closed.

In 1936 William H. Wesley, the sawmill owner who built the Wesley mansion in Point Washington, moved a small building he had used as an office and converted it into the first **Point Washington Post Office**. Later, about 1949, postmaster Helen Strickland wanted the post office to be closer to the home where she lived and cared for her mother. So she got permission and purchased another small building associated with the sawmill, a small cottage that had been used by the mill workers, and had it relocated to the corner of their property. That building, which still stands on the property, was in use until the post office closed about 10 years ago.

Several accounts say there was a **Grayton Store** and dance hall originally opened in the early 1900s and known as the White Elephant. Other accounts say the Grayton Store was built by the Butler family around 1937 and known as Butler General. According to these

The Grayton General Store (Florida State Archives Photographic Collection).

references, Van R. Butler, Sr. used wood salvaged from the Grayton Beach Hotel damaged in the 1936 hurricane. He may have then built a larger store in 1939. The store was popular during the late 1930s and early 1940s and apparently set records for the number of soft drinks sold. During World War II the United States Coast Guard established a station at Grayton Beach to patrol the beach and watch for German submarine activity, and the store was used in sustaining the troops. It was later bought and transformed into a restaurant called the Red Bar and Picolo's Restaurant, which opened in 1995 and continues in business.

The town of **Destin** was founded around 1835 by a New England fishing captain named Leonard Destin. Destin built fishing seines, boats manned by oars that pulled dragnets, and fished the area for decades with his descendants. He also recruited others and taught them his fishing techniques, leading to the operation of many fish camps in the area. By the 1930s captains such as William Marler were taking local residents on informal deep-sea fishing cruises. A couple named Colman and Mattie Kelly moved to the area and built a gas station and store, and in 1937 Kelly licensed his boat the *Martha-Gene* for sportfishing. Over the years more and more captains joined the ranks, and **Destin Harbor** now claims to have the largest charter fishing fleet in Florida. In 1948 they staged the first Destin Fishing Rodeo, and it has been held every year since.

The **Hang Out** in Panama City Beach was built in the late 1930s or early 1940s as an open-air snack bar and meeting and dance area at the **Long Beach Resort**, which J.E. Churchwell developed in the early 1930s. A photo of the Hang Out is included in Chapter 16. Unfortunately, the Hang Out was destroyed by Hurricane Eloise in 1975.

Snake-a-Torium opened in 1946, with snakes, an alligator, and various other animals. It was sold in 1991 to a local veterinarian and opened again in 1992, this time as **ZooWorld**. According to its website, ZooWorld is still open.

As noted in Chapter One, the forerunner of the **Seagrove Village Market** was built in 1949 by Seagrove Beach's founder, C.H. McGee, Sr. It has since evolved and has had several proprietors. According to its website, it closed for relocation in October 2015 and reopened in November 2016. A photo appears in Chapter Two.

Around 1952 Paul and Margaret Benedict bought 300 feet of Gulf-front land from C. H. McGee, Sr. and built two duplexes on it, followed by two more the next year. They named their eight kitchenette units **Seagrove Manor Hotel**. The Benedicts operated the hotel until 1967, when they sold it to T.E. Lord, and it was later owned and operated by the Flowers family. The original duplex arrangement was later expanded to include other buildings, and after some problems, it closed around 2007 and reopened with renovations in 2009. The name was also changed at some point to **Seagrove Villas Motel**. It finally closed for good in August 2012, and homes have been built where the long-time favorite once stood.

The Seagrove Manor and Villas Hotel from a postcard photo (postcard courtesy of Alice Forrester, used by permission of the Flowers family, Teri Gagliardi)

Soon after Paul and Margaret Benedict opened the Seagrove Manor Hotel around 1952 they added a coffee shop since there were no other places to eat in the area. When they sold the hotel and coffee shop in 1967, the new owner closed the coffee shop. But a restaurant known as the Seagrove Restaurant was established around 1972 by a subsequent owner, on the site of what later became the **Wheelhouse Restaurant**. The Wheelhouse was a local favorite for years before closing around 2012.

The **Gulfarium** opened in 1955 in Fort Walton Beach. Founded by a marine biologist interested in studying marine life in the Gulf of Mexico, the exhibits and shows were a way to generate enough income to support some of its other activities. The big tank originally housed several species of marine life including the dolphins, sharks, sea turtles, and rays. But later, a separate Living Sea exhibit was built for all the other species, so now the big tank is home only to the dolphins. Although they were traditionally called porpoises, these mammals are really Atlantic bottlenose dolphins. Being situated only

The Gulfarium in the 1960s (Florida State Archives Photographic Collection).

a stone's throw from the water, the facility was badly damaged by Hurricane Opal in 1995, but after major repairs it re-opened in 1996. The Gulfarium is still open, and active in marine research and conservation.

The Anderson family operated a fishing business on the downtown docks of St. Andrew Bay in Panama City. In 1956 they decided to move to Panama City Beach, and soon after that they opened **Capt. Anderson's Restaurant** at that location. In 1967 the Patronis family, also restaurateurs in Panama City, bought the restaurant and greatly expanded the size and profitability of the operation. It is one of the best-known restaurants in northwest Florida.

Museum of the Sea and Indian was located on US Highway 98 in Destin, and opened sometime in the 1950s. It certainly grabbed your attention as you drove by, with its wild advertisements and catchy signs. Although we often drove along that stretch of road, I don't remember my family ever stopping there. I can't find a current listing but one reference states that it was destroyed in 1995 by Hurricane Opal.

Miniature golf flourished after World War II, and **Goofy Golf** was the first example in the panhandle. It opened in 1958 in Fort Walton Beach, and featured concrete figures ranging from dinosaurs to elephants to sea monsters. It was based on a concept patented as "Tom Thumb Golf" in 1929. A very creative craftsman named Lee Koplin started out building figures for a course owner in California and eventually launched his own course called Goofy Golf in Mississippi. After Fort Walton Beach, courses were built in Pensacola and Panama City Beach, and imitators followed. Courses are still operating in those cities today.

I don't know when the first seafood restaurant opened in Destin but there have been many, and a few are consistently mentioned in lists of favorites. Dave Marler, a member of the longtime resident

Marler family, owned **Captain Dave's**. Although it was a favorite, it was never rebuilt after being destroyed by Hurricane Opal in 1995. Other members of the Marler family owned the **Blue Room**. The **Elephant Walk** in Sandestin has had many fans since first opening in 1985. It closed in 2003 but was re-established in 2013 by new owners. After several more years, it closed again. Finally, **Harbor Docks** was established in 1979 on the Destin harbor, and remains open.

Skyride arrived in Panama City Beach in the early 1960s. It featured a 100-foot-high gondola ride billed as the highest view available at the time, and attracted many visitors. Similar to a gondola lift that had operated at Disneyland since 1956, Skyride was erected on part of the land that had originally been purchased for construction of Goofy Golf. Although novel for a while, eventually buildings just as tall were built, and after the 200-foot-tall Miracle Strip Tower opened in 1966, Skyride didn't seem so spectacular. It was badly damaged by Hurricane Eloise in 1975, and never reopened.

The **Tombstone Territory** and **Petticoat Junction Amusement Parks** also opened in the early 1960s. Shortly after Goofy Golf opened in Panama City Beach a concessioner rented some of the property from Lee Koplin and opened a frontier train ride using miniature steam locomotives to ferry passengers into an area called the "Magic Forest". After noting the activity, Koplin eventually took over and built a complete western town that he called Tombstone Territory after a popular TV show. It featured a saloon, general store, jail, and other buildings, as well as concrete figures like those at Goofy Golf, except tailored to the western theme. About the same time Koplin was creating his western town, J.E. Churchwell also started operating a train ride at Long Beach Resort, and this full-size train took riders to a newly-constructed "Ghost Town". The resort had long featured some seasonal carnival rides, and eventually permanent rides were combined with the Ghost Town to form the park called Petticoat Junction. Both parks were successful for many years, but when the popularity of TV westerns began to wane, so did the parks. Tombstone

Territory closed around 1979, and Petticoat Junction called it quits on Labor Day 1984.

Arguably the most diverse of the attractions, **Miracle Strip Amusement Park** opened in 1963. The park was the brainchild of Jimmy Lark, whose family had successfully operated a group of cottages known as the Larkway Villas from the late 1930s to the mid-1960s. Lark and his partners built a monster roller coaster called the Starliner, claimed to be the fastest in the world. Rides such as a Ferris wheel and merry-go-round were gathered from other parks, and amusements included a haunted house and a water park. The Miracle Strip Amusement Park managed to stay ahead of the competition for decades, but had its last season in 2004, closing the day after Labor Day.

In 1966, the **Top O' the Strip** (aka **Miracle Strip Tower**) observation tower opened. This futuristic 200-foot tower provided incredible views to many before it was severely damaged by Hurricane Opal. It was finally demolished in 1995.

Eden Gardens State Park was created in 1968 after Lois Maxon donated the property and the Wesley mansion to the state. It is under the authority of the Florida Department of Environmental Protection and according to the website is open 365 days a year. See also the 'haunted house' in Chapter Five.

Grayton Beach State Park opened in 1968 after the Florida Board of Parks and Historic Memorials acquired much of the parcel of land in 1964. This park incorporates Western Lake, including the large part we 'discovered' in Chapter 10, and has picnic, camping, and boating facilities. According to the website it is open every day of the year.

The year 1973 marked the first opening of the resort known today as **Sandestin Golf and Beach Resort**. Built partly on land used during World War II to test captured German V-1 flying bombs, the resort has had several owners and managers on its way to becoming the sprawling complex it is today. The Hilton Sandestin Beach Golf Resort & Spa and The Village of Baytowne Wharf are just a few of the golf, dining, and beach attractions at Sandestin.

In 1981 developer Robert Davis founded the community of **Seaside** on 80 acres of land he inherited just west of Seagrove Beach. Although he at first envisioned a nostalgic beach town, the planning, layout, and architecture of Seaside soon came to embody what is called the "New Urbanism". The design, which was intended to reflect small-town life and to reduce urban sprawl, has become the model for hundreds of communities around the country. Many people who have not visited Seaside have nevertheless seen parts of it, since it was the setting for the 1998 movie "Truman Show" starring Jim Carrey. Despite some growing pains over the years and complaints that its homes are priced out of the reach of most homeowners, Seaside remains a desirable place to live and an important experiment in urban living.

Seaside town center area before the amphitheater and buildings were completed, circa 1984 (photo courtesy of Alice Forrester).

Deer Lake State Park opened in 1996, on land acquired by the Board of Trustees of the Internal Improvement Trust Fund of the State of Florida. This is the place where I loved to hike in the 1980s, and is still one of the most picturesque of the coastal dune lakes, although access to the dunes, woods, and lake is now restricted to designated walkways. It is open every day of the year.

The **Shops of Grayton**, an interesting collection of small art galleries and other stores, opened in 1998. The art and merchandise in these shops, ranges from oil and acrylic paintings, to glass mosaics and jewelry, to specialty food items. One of the galleries is covered in the later chapter on art at Seagrove Beach.

"Nobody goes there anymore. It's too crowded."
(Attributed to Yogi Berra)

Eighteen

Chapter 18. Chapter Two; Or the Saga of Hurricane Hall

"Though no one can go back and make a brand new start, anyone can start from now and make a brand new ending."   *(James R. Sherman)*

In 1951, as part of C.H. McGee, Sr.'s Third Addition to the original layout of Seagrove Beach, he built a Gulf-front four-bedroom house with a carport and an attached guest house. Over the years, it was owned by a moving and warehouse company and a couple of families, and somewhere along the line it acquired the name 'Hurricane Hall'. Looking back, Hurricane Hall was the first place my family stayed in Seagrove Beach. One year, back when we were taking annual vacations at motels in the Destin area, my parents decided instead to rent a house so we would have more room. The experience was memorable for less than the right reasons. The kitchen had a standard counter and also a long, high, wrap-around counter that served as a breakfast bar. When we walked in my mother was appalled at the condition of the countertops. The original Formica covering was badly worn in some spots and completely missing in others, and my mother considered it unacceptable for either eating or preparing food. But not to be outdone, she marshaled the supply of aluminum foil and covered the entire surface with foil, wrapped around the edge to keep it in place. It was definitely an unusual look for a kitchen, but it served the intended purpose, and we had a fun week. My mother was, also, not one to be deterred by small setbacks or appearances, and she quickly noticed the strong points of that house. It had views of the beach from almost all the rooms. And the floor plan was great, a split layout with two bedrooms, a hallway, and a bathroom on each side of the central living area. Each side could be completely closed off via a

The central living area of Hurricane Hall, which had four bedrooms in separate wings on each side.

door to the hallway. And each had a separate side door leading from the bathroom directly outside, to a walkway to the bluff. Many homes are now built with a split bedroom plan, but the design seemed pretty progressive for the 1950s, and was very efficient. The way it was split also meant heating and cooling could easily be zoned. The carport with attached guest house was located on a separate concrete slab near the road, and thus provided a fairly complete separate residence.

Our family continued visiting the area and my parents continued looking at real estate, and eventually they bought our first house in Seagrove Beach. We enjoyed that house all through the years my sister and I were in junior and senior high school. And after I left for college in New England I came back to visit my parents whenever possible and often headed to the beach to vacation. One day in 1969, while I was away at college, my mother was sitting at home in Montgomery having lunch when the phone rang. It was Cube McGee. Cube regularly arranged for repairs for my parents and talked to them about house-related matters, but this time it was something different. He explained that the owner of Hurricane Hall had passed away, and after a period of disagreement or indecision among family members, the fate of the property was now in the hands of an officer at a bank in Panama City. Some accounts of the status of the property had circulated, including stories about children or grandchildren gaining access to the locked house and 'camping out' there, even though the utilities had apparently been turned off. The house had a beautiful fireplace, so the kids apparently would go for a weekend in the off season and light a fire to provide warmth. But even though the family had ties to the place they apparently either didn't want to keep it, or couldn't agree on terms. Cube had gotten wind of the situation, so he asked my mother if she and my father might be interested in buying it, and gave her the contact information for the bank. My mother clearly remembered the house, and knew that although it needed some maintenance at the time we rented it, it had great potential. She understood the opportunity and knew it might not last, so she called my father at his office, explained the situation and got his blessing, and then drove the 3-1/2 hours to the bank in Panama City to give a deposit check to the bank official. After all the red tape for closing was completed they had bought the house from the decedent's estate.

Scrub oaks at Hurricane Hall.

At this time my parents still had our original house a few hundred feet up the road from Hurricane Hall, and that first house had been fixed up so it met all our needs. But my mother realized immediately that Hurricane Hall would make a great rental property, with its split 2 + 2 bedroom plan in the main house, and the guest house with bedroom next to the carport. It had a huge fireplace and a nice hearth, so even though we tended to associate the beach with summer vacations, it was a very nice place to spend Thanksgiving and Christmas holidays. My parents made some improvements such as converting the long screened porch, which ran the full 36 foot width of the house, into a glassed-in sun porch or Florida room. Because of the different building restrictions when the house was built, the porch was much closer to the bluff than homes that can be built today, so even though the house was all at ground level, the views were spectacular. It wasn't necessary back then to build a three- or four-story house to get good views. Eventually my parents sold the first house when an unusual offer came along, and the decision to sell was much easier since they owned the second home. So they began to use Hurricane Hall as their vacation home, and made more improvements.

Another thing we learned, mostly by accident, was that the house had acquired quite a reputation over the years, and it seemed like everyone knew the place. Although my parents had offered it for rent a limited amount in the 1970s, when they began to rent it out again in the 1980s and 1990s they found that people remembered it, and there were many repeat customers. Contractors and other locals also knew the house. I remember one time I was having some repair work done or something delivered, and I was giving directions, explaining to the person how CR 395 connected to CR 30-A, and how many houses were between a certain landmark, and so forth. When I ended by telling him that there was a sign on the house saying "Hurricane Hall", he immediately said "Oh, Hurricane Hall, why didn't you say so?!". From that point on I learned to always mention the name first, and in many cases I didn't need to continue with directions after that.

Hurricane Hall sign painted for me by Grayton artist Jim Poteet.

Although I left Alabama in the late 1960s, I found myself back in Montgomery in the mid-1980s because of family considerations. While there, I often went to Hurricane Hall, which my parents had been using less frequently because of illness. I reconnected with some relatives and some friends from school in Montgomery, and introduced this whole new group of people to the joys of Seagrove and Hurricane Hall. I got to know some new neighbors in Seagrove too, and made many new friends. Hurricane Hall became the center of our beach activities starting in the 1980s, and it will appear in other stories in later chapters.

Nineteen

Chapter 19. The Romance of Seagrove

"Tis better to have loved and lost, Than never to have loved at all."
(Alfred Lord Tennyson, "In Memoriam A. H. H.")

Ever since my parents bought the first house in 1962, Seagrove Beach was a labor, and a place, of love. My parents often let my sister and me invite friends to go there with us, and we would alternate weekends so as to keep the number of people manageable. When I joined the Boy Scouts, Seagrove turned out to be a good place to work on merit badges, whether for camping, camp cooking, building a fire, or hiking, so I sometimes took a friend who was in the Scouts to share in and certify my exploits. The beach was usually the first choice for any activities, but we also had plenty of forest nearby. There used to be an open roof structure on the beach in front of the house next door, and we called it the "sun shelter". It was like a small building with no walls, basically four big posts with a roof on top. I guess we were never satisfied to do things the normal way, or to use the structure as it was originally designed. So one time when we wanted to camp on the beach, we decided to sleep on top of the shelter rather than under it. I seem to remember getting quite wet that night from both dew and the spray from the Gulf, but at least we didn't roll off the roof during the night.

The sun shelter we used as a camping spot.

My sister never had a problem finding friends to go with her, and although they were more into swimming, shopping, and girl talk, they found as many things to do as my friends and I. My parents also routinely loaned the house to their friends, never asking anything in return. But even though they didn't expect anything, the friends would usually figure out ways to show their appreciation. One man always fixed or improved something at the house, like the screen door on the back porch that was always breaking. We had replaced various hinges, springs, handles, and whatnot, but always had a problem with that door. That is, until he replaced it with one better suited for that environment, so we were amply rewarded. In another case I remember an unexpected delivery arrived one day at our house in Montgomery, and it was a very nice state-of-the-art barbecue grill. Other friends who had vacation houses at places like Lake Martin or Gulf Shores in Alabama sometimes reciprocated by letting our family stay at their places.

Occasionally our family would go to Seagrove for a vacation with another family, and their kids would grow to love the place as much as we did. I remember one case in which some of my parents' friends had kids several years younger than my sister and me. Although naturally we were into different activities, we helped take care of the younger kids and it all worked out well. That family went down again on their own after I went away to college, when their kids were in high school. I had an opportunity to reconnect with the family over 20 years later when I went back to Montgomery, and about that time my father told me a story that was hard to forget. It seems that the daughter had grown up and gotten married, but had a particularly painful divorce a few years later. Her father had been trying to help her get over it and one day he asked her if there was anything he could do to ease the pain. Even though she probably hadn't been there in years, she told him the best thing he could do was to drive her to Seagrove sometime, just for a day. So they picked a time and he drove her there. He waited in the car because she wanted to just go sit on the beach by herself. After a couple of hours she came back to the car and told him she was ready to go home and get on with her life. That's the kind of calming influence Seagrove has on people.

Seagrove sunset with an unusual cloud pattern.

Of course relatives were always welcome at Seagrove, too. One of my uncles was in the Air Force and stationed in different parts of the country at various times. But for awhile he was assigned to Maxwell Air Force Base in Montgomery, so we got to see more of him and his wife. He had us out to the base to see the aircraft he flew, and would pay me to wash his new Chevrolet Impala. They sometimes went to Seagrove with us, and my biggest thrill was once when I was 12 or 13 and we were all driving down to the beach house. I got to ride with him in his fully customized Volkswagen camper bus with beautiful wood paneling and cabinets.

Sometimes my mother took her bridge club to Seagrove for a ladies' weekend. They played bridge every week in Montgomery, usually had two tables, and the group was made up of the wives of men who worked with my father, the wife of his attorney, some neighbors, and some old friends. They had all known each other for a long time and thoroughly enjoyed each other's company. So what better way to spend a weekend than playing bridge while enjoying the beach! I'm sure they played a lot of bridge, but they also spent time doing other things, and we'll never know the details of all the fun they had. These were of course responsible, dedicated, loving, middle-aged wives and mothers, but the photo below shows what effect Seagrove can have on the mind and spirit of even the most dedicated family members. That's a package of lemons in her hand - I'm not sure what those were for, but I think I see a blender on the counter. The names and faces have been obscured to protect the innocent....

Bridge club members in beach vacation garb.

I had a friend in junior high and high school who shared my interests in music, coin collecting, and other things, so naturally he was one of the people I picked to go to Seagrove with us. Like everyone else, he was fond of the place, and he couldn't wait to get back each time. My parents didn't really know the boy's parents except through me, but one year when I was in high school they learned somehow that the boy's father was going to have an operation and was facing a convalescence of several weeks. Figuring he would do better in a relaxing atmosphere and away from home and distractions, they offered the couple our house at Seagrove. I don't know the couple's ages at the time, but their son (my friend) was about 14, and he was definitely an 'only child'. That is, until the parents went to Seagrove. Even though the father was in bed convalescing from a painful operation, we learned a few weeks later that my friend, who was already in high school, was going to have a sibling. The baby was healthy and the parents were ecstatic, but for the former 'only child' life was quite different. After being accustomed to all the attention, he took it pretty hard when his parents had to devote all their time to his new baby brother. I remember the problems he had in high school and his general change in attitude. His parents, of course, still loved him, but the newborn at home complicated everything. It got so bad that at one point he ran away from home. He had for years had a 'paper route', delivering local newspapers on his bicycle to earn money, so he was a very strong cyclist. And that helped explain his idea for running away. After authorities checked with friends and searched locally, my mother told me that the Highway Patrol found him on his bicycle on the highway leading south out of Montgomery, halfway to the city of Luverne, which is about 50 miles from Montgomery. I'm not sure his exact goal was ever determined, but we quickly figured that he probably had his sights set on one place that would have represented peace and happiness - Seagrove.

One last anecdote took me a little by surprise. You read earlier the story of Hurricane Hall, the first place we ever stayed in Seagrove, and which became our second house there. And later in the chapter on art in the area you'll read about a doctor from Montgomery who decided to pursue his passion for art along the Gulf Coast. Well, that same artist once explained to me that his family also stayed at Hurricane Hall at least once as they came to love the area. They started when his kids were growing up, and eventually bought their own place. And during a stay at Hurricane Hall, while his son was visiting from college in New England, the son went to a party one night in Destin and met a girl named Dolly, whom he would eventually marry. Maybe that was just luck, or maybe it's another example of the effect this area has on people. The couple is still together as of this writing.

Twenty

Chapter 20. Starry Nights and Photographing Halley's Comet

"I often think that the night is more alive and more richly colored than the day." *(Vincent Van Gogh)*

My father introduced me to the night sky when I was a boy in Montgomery, and I've remained fascinated by the stars all my life, ultimately working in the field of astronomy. Since there were few lights in the Seagrove area as compared to a city, the skies were very dark and there were many more stars visible. In addition, having an ocean on one side of the community meant no light coming from that direction, and the ocean horizon made it easier to see objects low in the sky to the south. So any kind of star gazing, whether with the naked eye, or sitting on a lawn chair with a pair of binoculars, or using an amateur telescope, was rewarding. I observed from Seagrove all through high school, looking at the moon and planets, galaxies and nebulae, unusual stars, and meteors. When I went away to college I didn't get to the beach as often, but always went during the summers.

Later, after my parents bought Hurricane Hall and I moved back to Montgomery for a while in the mid 1980s, I started going back to Seagrove and took an amateur telescope. The skies were already dark and the southern horizon was perfect, but at that point I wanted to block out both the wind and any light from other houses, so I came up with the idea of hanging some sort of baffles on two sides of the area of the yard where I set up the telescope. That way the house would be to the north, the baffles on both sides, and the clear ocean horizon to the south. I thought my old friend John Fonville might have some tarps, and so went to talk to him and explained what I was trying to do. Sure enough, he had just the thing – some very heavy canvas tarps that he kept folded up in his shed. He told me if they would work not to even ask each time I arrived on Friday night for a weekend, but to just take them from the shed and return them when I was done. So I scrounged around for some metal pipe used in making chain-link fences that I figured would make good vertical poles, and I inserted those in pipe sleeves sunk into the ground. Having the sleeves in the

The yard at Hurricane Hall, where I set up the telescope, using heavy canvas tarps around it to block the wind and neighboring lights.

ground meant I could easily install the poles when I was going to put up the tarps, and then remove them when I was finished so there was nothing sticking up in the yard. Once the poles were in place in the yard, I ran a rope from an eye bolt at the top of each pole to another eye bolt screwed into the eave of the house, and hung the tarps over the ropes. The tarps were not like ordinary tent canvas but much heavier, so once they were hung on the ropes they did not blow around in the wind, especially when I used some bricks to weight down the bottom edges. With the scope set up in the yard and the tarps on both sides I was sheltered from the wind and any surrounding lights, and had many good nights looking at stars, planets, galaxies, and other objects.

Seeing that I liked to observe the night sky, the couple that lived next door to Hurricane Hall once asked me if I had been to the observatory near Seagrove. Most professional observatories are on mountaintops and often in remote places, and I wasn't aware of anything like that in northwest Florida. They told me it was located near Eastern Lake, was called the "South Walton Astronomical Observatory", and was operated by a man they knew from their church. I was naturally interested to see what was going on that close to my house, so they arranged for me to talk to their friend. Back in the 1980s the area between Eastern Lake and Deer Lake was only beginning to be developed and what I found when I drove down Lakeshore Drive was, in fact, a sign on a fence marking the observatory. My neighbor's friend was a retired professor from North Carolina who had become interested in astronomy. Once he retired he devoted most of his time to observing for an organization that guides amateur astronomers in certain types of observations, and makes their results available to professional astronomers. He used a dark spot between some dunes where he had built a wood platform for observing and a small building next to it to store his telescope. Although hardly a traditional observatory, it nevertheless served its purpose, and he spent years there making many useful observations for the organization.

Every year or so you'll see a story on the news about a comet that's visible, maybe through binoculars, if you know just where to look. Occasionally one is visible to the unaided eye, but really bright ones are very rare. Comets are solar system bodies formed of ice, dust, and rocky particles and were once famously described by an astronomer as being like "dirty snowballs". Most comets travel in cigar-shaped orbits many times the size of the earth's orbit, and most take many years, sometimes hundreds of years, to make just one orbit. Comets have a small nucleus no more than a few miles in diameter, and are quite dark during most of their orbits when they are far from the sun. However, as they approach the sun, the sun's radiation heats the surface of the nucleus and causes certain materials to essentially "boil off", spewing out gas and dust that together form a sort of atmosphere around the nucleus. This atmosphere, called a coma, is much larger than the nucleus, and can be thousands of miles in diameter. Perhaps the most spectacular part of a comet, though, and the part from which it gets its name, is the tail. In certain rare cases a comet's tail can extend in a long arc across the sky, making a truly memorable sight. But like the coma, the tail doesn't even form unless the comet is close enough to the sun for the radiation to produce a coma, which in some cases then gets blown out into a tail by the sun's radiation. Actually, comets have two tails, one of gas and the other of dust, pointing in slightly different directions. Even though in photos comets look like they're speeding along with their long tail streaming out behind, in fact they appear motionless in the sky when observed, and the tail always points away from the sun. So when a comet is traveling away from the sun in its orbit, the tail is actually streaming out in front of the comet's nucleus, pushed out by the sun's radiation.

By far the best known comet, and one that's been observed for over two thousand years, is Halley's Comet. It last passed the earth in 1986 and was viewed by millions of people the world over. Although observed by ancient astronomers as early as 240 B.C., those viewers didn't realize they were witnessing the return of an object that had been visible at an earlier time. It wasn't until 1705 that English astronomer Edmund Halley determined that the comet was traveling in an orbit that brought it back near the earth at intervals of about 76 years, and based on that, he predicted its next appearance. So, although the comet had been observed many times before, it was named after

Halley. Sadly, he did not live to see his prediction come true, since he died 16 years before its return in 1758. When seen in 1910, the comet traveled particularly close to earth, which even passed through the comet's tail. I mentioned earlier that comets can take hundreds of years to complete an orbit around the sun, while the earth takes only one year. Why does it take a comet so long to go around? The diagram below shows the orbit of Halley's Comet superimposed on the orbits of the planets. As you can see, the orbit is long and narrow, and takes Halley out beyond the orbit of Neptune. So the reason it takes Halley so long to complete the trip is that it's a huge orbit. Incidentally, right now the comet is almost at its greatest distance from the sun, way out beyond the orbit of Neptune. In a few years it will start the long trek back toward the sun for its next rendezvous with the earth. But back to 1986. The close approach by Halley in 1910 meant the comet was

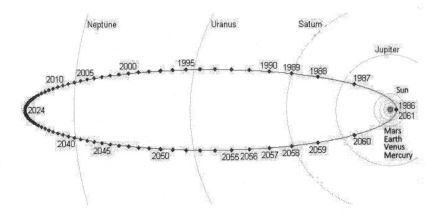

Diagram of the orbit of Halley's comet showing the orbits of the planets and the comet's position each year.

spectacularly bright, and so amateur and professional astronomers alike were anxious to see it during the return of 1985-86.

Capturing an image of a comet can be tricky because even though a telescope gathers a lot more light than the unaided eye and makes objects look brighter, the patch of sky visible through a telescope is so small that you can't see much of the comet's tail. So I used a film camera by itself, but mounted it on a telescope or motor-driven mount so that it could follow the comet during each exposure. The 1986 visit was not a particularly good one as the comet was barely visible to the unaided eye, but I was able to capture the photo below from the bluff at Seagrove Beach. The photo was taken while the comet was approaching the sun. In the following months it passed behind the sun and then began its long journey to the outer solar system in its cigar-shaped orbit.

Halley's comet showing extended tail, photographed from the bluff at Seagrove.

In addition to Comet Halley providing an interesting object for me to photograph in 1986, that year marked the first time a comet had been observed up close by a spacecraft from earth. The European Space Agency sent a probe named Giotto to within less than 400 miles of the comet's nucleus and captured the first closeup photos. Amazingly, the nucleus, which provides the material that can stretch into a tail tens of millions of miles long, is only a few miles across, shaped a little like a peanut. As shown in the photo below, the surface of the nucleus is very dark in color, essentially black. But the photo also shows "jets" where bright gas and dust are boiling off the surface due to heating by the sun. That gas and dust forms the comet's coma and tail, and the dust makes it hard to capture a photograph when approaching close to the nucleus because it obscures the target.

The nucleus of Halley's Comet, photographed by the European Space Agency's Giotto spacecraft in 1986 (ESA).

Although you won't be able to see Halley's Comet again until it circles around the sun in the year 2061, each year in April and May and again in October and November you can actually see tiny fragments of the comet - in the form of meteors. The meteor shower in the spring is called the Eta Aquarids, named after a constellation in the sky, and the shower in the fall is called the Orionids, also named after a constellation. Comets leave a trail of dust all along their orbits, so even though the comet itself is only bright when it passes near the earth and the sun every 76 years, the earth passes the comet's orbit twice each year, as shown in the figure.

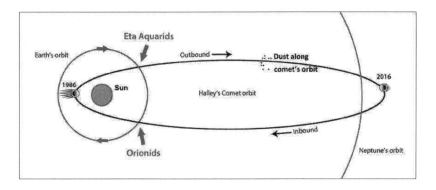

Diagram of the orbit of Halley's Comet, showing how the earth crosses the orbit twice each year, passing through dust left by the comet, and leading to meteor showers in the earth's atmosphere.

Whether or not the comet itself is there, twice a year some of those tiny specs of dust burn up in the earth's atmosphere, and those are the meteors we see. So even if you missed the famous visit in 1986, or won't be around to see it when it returns in 2061, you can see a little bit of Halley's Comet each year if you know where to look.

Twenty-one

Chapter 21. Art at Seagrove Beach

"Every child is an artist. The problem is how to remain an artist once we grow up."   (Pablo Picasso)

As picturesque as the beaches of northwest Florida are, it's only natural that artists are drawn to the area. The emerald green water, the sugar-white sand, the dunes, the sea oats, and a variety of marine animals, all provide interesting subjects for an artist's photograph or painting. And at Seagrove Beach the gnarled scrub oak trees provide another unusual combination of form and color. A survey of all the art and artists that may have been influenced by the region is beyond the scope of this chapter, but an internet search will certainly produce listings for many shops and galleries in the area today. My purpose here is to highlight a few instances where Seagrove and the surrounding areas were an inspiration to some.

Soon after we started going regularly to the first house at Seagrove, my parents noticed some captivating oil paintings shown in a few places in the area. They also often saw one artist setting up and painting along the bluff and on CR 30-A. Her name was Mary Bruns, and the three soon became friends.

Scrub oaks at Grayton Beach painted by Mary Bruns (photo courtesy of Maunsel White).

According to a biography posted online, Mary Bryan Bruns was born in New Jersey in 1905, and moved to New Orleans as a child. She studied to become an artist but worked as a journalist for several years. After writing and illustrating feature articles for the *New Orleans Times Picayune*, she later worked as a copywriter and editor for the advertising department of the *New Orleans Item* from 1946 until 1955. She moved to Seagrove in 1961 and resumed her career as an artist, using oils and watercolors. She was drawn to the subtle appearance, variety, and changing nature of the coastal environment, and devoted most of her time to recording the beauty of the area. Although she sold some of her paintings, her family owns most of her work.

The Gulf painted by Mary Bruns (photo courtesy of Maunsel White).

The reproductions shown here are of paintings that have been exhibited in the area at various times. They demonstrate Ms. Bruns' devotion to, and mastery of, presenting the rich colors, the textures, and the scenes that help make Seagrove Beach and the surrounding area unique. Another of her paintings appears in Chapter 14.

Some years after Mary Bruns began painting in Seagrove Beach, folks in Grayton Beach began gathering every year to exhibit, buy, and sell art. A festival called the *Grayton Beach Fine Arts Festival* started in 1989 and included works from individual local artists, as well as from early galleries like *Ideas* and *The Gallery in Grayton*. The content ranged from oil paintings and pottery to furniture and stained glass. One artist who became very popular partly as a result of the festival was a retired physician from Montgomery named Jim Poteet. The photo below shows just how 'rustic' the surroundings were in the festival's early years, when artists set up their work next to their vehicles along the sand roads of Grayton. By 2010 the name of the festival had changed to the *ArtsQuest Fine Arts Festival* and it was located in Seaside. By 2017 the event was held in Sandestin and advertised original art from over 150 artists from around the country.

The Grayton Beach Fine Arts Festival, 1990s (photo courtesy of Dr. Jim Poteet).

I introduced our second home, Hurricane Hall, in an earlier chapter. Many years after the Grayton festival started I happened upon a local artist and source of art quite by accident, when having some repairs done on the home. Many homes around the beach or with pools are designed with a direct outside door from a bathroom to allow easy access to and from the water. Hurricane Hall was designed exactly like that, and, in fact, had a bathroom on each side of the house that opened directly onto a side walkway leading to the bluff and the beach. The elements being what they are next to the ocean, those wood doors got an awful lot of weathering, not to mention a lot of direct traffic. So after patching them a couple of times they finally needed to be replaced. They were an odd size, only about two feet wide by about six feet tall. I think the contractor had to special order the replacements or have them custom built. But whatever, he purchased the new doors and removed the old ones and set them in the carport along with other materials to be discarded. One day I came back from shopping to meet with the contractor, and was surprised that the old doors were no longer there. When I asked him about it, the contractor said something like "Oh, the man came and picked them up." When I asked who the man was, the contractor mentioned that the guy who picked them up had something to do with an art gallery, and he thought I knew about it. It turns out I didn't know anything about it and was curious who would want some old, broken, mildewing wooden doors. But the comment about an art gallery gave me a lead. I remembered visiting a little collection of stores and galleries called the *Shops of Grayton* in Grayton Beach, so I called over to one of them and eventually tracked down the doors.

The Shops Of Grayton are home to many types of artwork. (rendering courtesy of Dr. Jim Poteet).

It seems that the owner of one of the shops, who was also an artist, had noticed the doors sitting out near the road while driving by and knew he could clean them up a little and use them as surfaces for the sort of mural artwork he did. The contractor knew the doors were just going to be thrown away, so he let the man take them. The shop owner was none other than Jim Poteet, the retired physician who had enjoyed visiting Grayton Beach when he lived in Montgomery, and who got his start at the *Grayton Beach Fine Arts Festival*. In 1993 he decided to open a studio in Grayton, and he later built a group of eight small modular units to be used as studios or stores. The *Shops of*

Grayton, as the complex was called, opened on Logan Lane in Grayton Beach in 1998, and *The Studio* was Jim Poteet's gallery.

Brightly-painted furniture by James Poteet (photo courtesy of Dr. Jim Poteet).

When I first reached Jim, I jokingly accused him of stealing my doors, even though I knew we were discarding them. He played along with me, and then offered that if I would let him keep the doors as painting materials he would paint me a custom wood sign for Hurricane Hall. That sounded fair, so I agreed. A few weeks later I visited *The Studio* and recognized one of the doors, now a bright, colorful, watercolor mural. Both eventually sold and I'm sure made the perfect addition to the walls of a beach house. Eventually he brought me the Hurricane Hall sign shown in the photo in Chapter 18. And, in the end, the old bathroom doors found a much better home than the local landfill they were originally destined for.

Twenty-two

Chapter 22. Sunday Mornings at Deer Lake

"Heaven is under our feet as well as over our heads." (Henry David Thoreau, "Walden")

After my move back to Montgomery in the mid-1980s, I often went to Seagrove for the weekend to relax and unwind. Depending on the season, I might swim, walk the beach, star gaze, read, or work on the house. But regardless of the other activities, if the weather was good I liked to spend Sunday mornings at Deer Lake before driving back to Montgomery. This was long before the Deer Lake State Park was created, and there were few markings for it along CR 30-A, no parking areas, and no cleared areas. Although there were already quite a few houses around Eastern Lake and the smaller lakes east of it, there was no development directly around Deer Lake. Since I enjoyed hiking in the quiet forest around Deer Lake, I liked the area east of the lake, on the opposite side from Eastern Lake, best. At that time CR 30-A extended east for several miles all the way to Hwy 98, and a few narrow dirt roads on the south side of CR 30-A headed into the forest. I would pick one of these, park my car on the shoulder, and walk down the dirt road into the trees. The forest, mostly southern pine like slash pine, is high and dry along the road, and as I walked further from the road I'd pass palmetto, mushrooms, and several other types of ground cover such as lichens. A common type of lichen I saw is often referred to as Reindeer lichen, named for its importance as a foodstuff in much colder climates. It's also called Deer moss. Even though they look a lot like plants, lichens are actually not plants. They're a symbiotic association of algae, or blue-green bacteria, and fungi. Symbiotic means they live together without harm to either, and usually for mutual benefit. So if they're not plants, they must be animals, right? No, they're not animals either. Even though lichens are formed from two different organisms, neither organism is quite plant or animal, as neither algae nor fungi are members of the plant or animal kingdoms of life. Even though it usually grows on the ground, Deer moss has no

Deer moss, a type of lichen that grows near Deer Lake (photo courtesy of Wikimedia Commons).

roots, and gets all its water from rain, dew, and moisture in the air. It grows very slowly, and feels anywhere from prickly when the air and surroundings are dry, to soft when it's humid.

After I had walked a ways, the road or path disappeared into a swampy area that extends east from the lake. Depending on the season and recent rain conditions, I could have difficulty crossing this wet area, but was usually helped along by boards or branches in the lowest spots that made it possible to get through. Once I was in the swampy area, the trees and bushes became so thick you couldn't tell how far the water extended. It was humid and close, a distinct ecosystem completely different from the pine forest. The plants were different from those found in the forest, and the shallow water harbored small creatures. After continuing further in the swampy area, with no warning the thicket suddenly parted and I would find myself facing a fairly steep sand bank, maybe four to six feet high, which marked the beginning of the dunes. Once I scaled the embankment a vast stretch of dunes opened out before me. There was so much variety -- all shapes and sizes, standing alone or in groups.

Dunes near Deer Lake.

Some dunes were almost purely the sugar-white sand, while others had vegetation covering them, either grasses or low shrubs, or scrub oak trees on the peak that looked decades old. Each one had its own history and, I'm sure, a story to tell. I found it one of the most peaceful and relaxing spots in a region known for those characteristics. I kept an eye out for unusual objects, like driftwood, shell casings, or Indian pottery. But mostly I just walked and dreamed.

And bordering the dunes was the lake itself, with its dark-colored water and gentle waves, its grasses and lily pads, its birds and other animals. As I discussed earlier, these rare coastal dune lakes are fed mostly from streams, rainfall, and groundwater seepage from the uplands and the Gulf. Like the other lakes, Deer Lake has a natural

Water lilies on Deer Lake.

channel that opens intermittently, connecting it to the Gulf. Depending on factors such as rainfall, other inflows, and the water level of the

Gulf, the freshwater of the lake sometimes flows into the Gulf, and at other times saltwater from the Gulf flows into the lake. The water is usually tea-colored or black due to dissolved organic matter. Although not as large as its neighbors Eastern Lake and Camp Creek Lake, Deer Lake has always been special, the quiet one, the lake with the lily pads and grasses along its peaceful undeveloped shores. Fortunately, due to the foresight of the Internal Improvement Trust Fund of the State of Florida, Deer Lake and the land around it were acquired by the state starting in 1996 and designated a state park. You can see most of what I've described today from a beautiful wood walkover leading out from the parking area in the state park, but you don't get the effect of the change in topography and conditions as the pine forest transitions to the dense wetlands. You don't get to be immersed in the marsh and then suddenly burst upon the sand embankment. You don't get to walk right in the dunes, and to examine each minute detail. It's still wonderful today, but you don't feel the same intimate rapport with nature you could get back then. After my walk and maybe some time sitting in the dunes I would slowly work my way back out, retracing steps through each of the environments and gradually returning to civilization. It was sometimes hard to leave, but I was always better prepared for the coming week after my Sunday mornings at Deer Lake.

Twenty-three

Chapter 23. Hurricane Opal

*"The little reed, bending to the force of the wind, soon stood upright
again when the storm had passed over."*   *(Aesop)*

The 1995 Atlantic hurricane season was an unusually active
one, with a total of 19 named storms, including 11 hurricanes, of
which five were major hurricanes reaching Category 3 or higher. In
early September an area of low pressure known as a Tropical Wave
formed off the west coast of Africa. Unremarkable at first, it crossed
the central Atlantic and Caribbean over the next two weeks and
merged with a low-pressure area over the western Caribbean on
September 23. It didn't even reach the status of a tropical depression
until it arrived at the east coast of the Yucatan Peninsula on September
27. Finally, on September 30, it was named Tropical Storm Opal,
becoming the fifteenth named storm and ninth hurricane of the season.
It reached hurricane status on October 2, and then strengthened rapidly
on October 3 and 4, reaching Category 4 with sustained winds of 150
mph. It weakened slightly before making landfall on October 4 west
of Fort Walton Beach, near the Okaloosa-Santa Rosa County line, as
a Category 3 storm. Although sustained winds of 115-125 mph are
enough to do major damage, the National Weather Service wrote that

Opal's legacy would always be the devastating storm surge that inundated the western panhandle.

Storm surge of 10-15 feet was reported from Navarre Beach to Destin, and may have reached 20 feet near Miramar Beach. A surge of six to eight feet was observed even in the inland bays from Pensacola to Choctawhatchee Bay. One section of US 98 about a half-mile long between Destin and Fort Walton Beach was destroyed, turning what was once part of Santa Rosa Island into an inlet of Choctawhatchee Bay. And a large area of infrastructure such as water, sewer, phone, and electric systems was damaged along with many thousands of homes and other structures.

Satellite photo of Hurricane Opal from the NOAA.

I traveled to the area a few weeks later, and although I knew the damage to the beach would be severe, I didn't know the extent of the damage to homes in the area. I knew that Hurricane Hall had survived because a friend I called told me she had driven by and that the damage was not severe. The home had suffered only moderate damage to the shingles on the south and east sides of the roof nearest the Gulf. However, what I found next door was another story, and it took my breath away. A retired couple had lived in the house year-round for many years, and I had known them since at least the mid-

1980s. The house had been built in the 1970s, roughly 20 years after the original homes, and was of typical frame construction with a red brick veneer and a massive fireplace and chimney in the living room. The husband had passed away the previous year and the wife had moved to a care facility only a few months before the storm, so the home was unoccupied. When I walked over I saw that the porch on the front of the house had been demolished, the front brick wall had been blown into the living room, and the massive chimney had been broken, lifted up, and tilted at an angle. The roof had been completely removed and blown upside-down onto the roof of the house to the west. That next house, although it appeared to be relatively untouched by the storm, had a condemned notice on it, apparently because of the roof lying on top of it. It was altogether an amazing sight.

The south side of the neighbor's house with brick wall blown into the living area and the roof gone.

These photos show the extent of the destruction. All this damage, a home almost completely destroyed by wind, occurred only about 25 feet from Hurricane Hall. Was it due to a difference in construction materials or methods? Although we always thought of the cinder block construction of the 1950s as very durable, the brick walls of the neighboring house were also substantial. Hurricanes are known to spawn a large number of tornadoes around them, and those tornadoes can cause extreme local damage in small areas. My guess is that a tornado touched down in the area, producing winds and pressure differentials powerful enough to remove the roof and blow down walls only 25 feet away, while miraculously sparing our home. Hurricane Hall would ultimately live to see many more storms.

The roof of the neighbor's house, which was blown intact onto the house next door to theirs.

Although the bluff at Seagrove is almost 40 feet high and has offered protection from waves and storm surges for centuries, it was not immune to the wave action and surge of a storm like Opal. When the original homes in Seagrove Beach were built, C.H. McGee, Sr. and Cube built a series of stairways to the beach, forming and pouring them from solid concrete so they would be permanent and not require maintenance. In the following years some were modified with wood stairs over the original concrete, often with wide landings and sometimes benches partway down the slope. Although the newer stairways had nice handrails and looked good, they were no match for a storm like Opal. The concrete stairs had survived earlier storms that could wash away wood stairs, but even those gave way when sections of the bluff were washed away by the hurricane.

View of the bluff from the beach showing the remains of a stairway. The section at the bottom is concrete.

After sizing up the situation at Seagrove Beach and making sure the house was secure for the time being I drove toward Destin to see what damage had occurred in other areas. The photos I took give a glimpse of the destruction.

Destruction in Destin.

A building destroyed in Destin.

Naming of North Atlantic hurricanes is controlled by the World Meteorological Organization, which alternates between six lists of names for a particular year. Because of the severity of Opal and the damage it caused, the name has been retired from the lists, and will never be used again.

Twenty-four

Chapter 24. Where Did All Those Names Come From?

> *"What's in a name? that which we call a rose*
> *By any other name would smell as sweet."* *(William*
> *Shakespeare, "Romeo and Juliet").*

In almost any reference to the Florida Panhandle and Walton or adjacent counties you'll find a term like "Miracle Strip", or "Emerald Coast", or something about how beautiful the beaches are. One of the earliest amusement parks in the area was named the Miracle Strip Amusement Park. And the newer part of Highway 98 east of Destin is named the Emerald Coast Parkway. So where did all these names come from, and what names apply to which places? As you might expect there's no simple answer, but here's a rundown on some of the most widely-known monikers.

The earliest of these names or phrases I found is the description "World's most beautiful bathing beaches", which was coined by J.E. Churchwell for his Long Beach Resort. The resort was being developed in the mid-1930s and the name must have come along at about the same time. Many postcards and photos from the 1940s, 1950s, and 1960s use the phrase, although I've seen it shortened to

"World's most beautiful beaches" in later references to such places as Fort Walton Beach and Panama City Beach. Starting in 1946 the area around Destin and Fort Walton was often referred to as the "Playground Area of Northwest Florida", or simply the "Playground", and the Fort Walton Beach newspaper was at one time called the *Playground News*, and later the *Playground Daily News*. As with other descriptive words or phrases, this one apparently had more than one form and was sometimes applied to a larger area.

Then in 1952 local writer Claude Jenkins coined the term "Miracle Strip". Jenkins wrote a column called "Town Crier" in the *Playground News*, the local paper, and was known as a very creative writer, not afraid to be bold, elegant, and even sarcastic when the occasion warranted. But according to one source he first used the new phrase in a weekly paper in DeFuniak Springs called *The Breeze*. One day he was driving west on old US Highway 98, the one that followed fairly close to the beach in many places, and came over a hill and out of a wooded area. As he came upon the shoreline, with its sparkling water and snow-white sand, he has said he was so impressed by the beauty of it all that he thought it must be a miracle. Some locals are convinced the place where Jenkins had his epiphany was about eight miles east of Destin on a stretch of road at Miramar Beach. Apparently the hill was known locally as Yellow Dunes, and it may be where today the newer portion of US 98 veers off and heads inland, while the old road continues toward the beach. After Jenkins articulated his feeling with the phrase Miracle Strip, many establishments adopted the name, and part of US 98 between Destin and Fort Walton is now called the Miracle Strip Parkway. In March of 1956 officials from several business associations officially adopted the term to represent a 100-mile stretch of US 98's businesses from Pensacola to Panama City.

A few years before Claude Jenkins had his revelation, and about 15 miles to the east, developer C.H. McGee, Sr also fell in love with the view of the Gulf of Mexico from the panhandle. As described in Chapter One, in 1949 McGee bought land that the Seagrove Company had been trying to develop. He kept the name, but put his own vision into the development. He coined the phrase "Where Nature Did Its Best" and used it on signs advertising land for sale in Seagrove Beach. The original name Seagrove was probably chosen to commemorate the thick grove of scrub oak and other trees on the high bluff. On a humorous note, some residents have written that in the early days when visitors were sparse in the off-season, or maybe all year around, they used to mock Seagrove. One Grayton resident wrote that she and her girlfriends would occasionally hike down the beach to Seagrove, which was so deserted they called it Seagrave. The figure shows part of the letterhead Cube McGee used for his real estate company, where he again used the phrase his father had come up with years earlier.

Original letterhead from Seagrove Beach Realty using the phrase "Where Nature Did Its Best".

New York Times columnist Howell Raines is credited with coining the phrase "Redneck Riviera". The phrase has been widely used, with a wide range of intentions, in addition to being the subject of whole books. In 1978 he wrote an article entitled "Todd and Stabler Offseason Game: Living It Up on 'Redneck Riviera'" in which he described how National Football League quarterbacks Richard Todd and Kenny Stabler used to unwind in Gulf Shores, Alabama, after a grueling season in the NFL. The wealthy, famous young athletes could live anywhere they wanted, but chose to spend the off-season in L.A. – that's short for "Lower Alabama", of course, and is what some residents humorously called the resort town of Gulf Shores. And although the phrase "Redneck Riviera" is usually ascribed to Raines, he says in the article that it's actually a term some Alabama wags use for that stretch of beach. In this case I think "Wags" means wives and girlfriends. But even though Raines may not have coined the phrase, he probably deserves a lot of credit for spreading knowledge of it in his writing.

According to a local newspaper in Fort Walton, about five years later a junior high school student named Andrew Dier came up with the name "Emerald Coast" for a 1983 contest, and won $50 for his effort. The term was originally meant to apply to Okaloosa and Walton Counties. But a year later it was expanded to include the town of Navarre and Navarre Beach, which are in Santa Rosa County. And by 1998 it was being applied to the coast all the way from Pensacola to Panama City. In 2011 the Greater Fort Walton Beach Chamber of Commerce argued that the use should be restricted to Okaloosa County, which includes Fort Walton. But by then so many establishments were using the term that it seemed impossible to roll back the usage, and attorneys have advised the Tourism Development Council that it's just too generic a term. So it appears you'll continue to see this term applies to a long strip of beach for the foreseeable future.

Other names and slogans ranging from "The Beach" to "The Beaches of South Walton" to "Florida's Great Northwest" have come along, with some quite durable to this day. But let's end with another phrase with an interesting origin. As we've seen earlier, the town of Destin was founded by a fisherman, thrived originally on fishing, and still derives a major portion of its fame and revenue from fishing. So it's fitting that the town's nickname should center on fishing, and it does. It's known as the "World's Luckiest Fishing Village", and the story behind that phrase involves Leroy Collins, who was Florida's governor in the mid-1950s. Local charter boat captain Reddin 'Salty' Brunson convinced the governor to take a short, 20-minute ride around the harbor. And by the time they returned Collins had caught a 29-pound king mackerel. When a reporter commented that it was pretty hard to believe he could have returned with such a big fish, Collins merely replied "Not in Destin, the luckiest fishing village in the world." The name became official in October, 1956, and has stuck ever since. So - what's in a name? For this special stretch of coastline it's pretty much whatever inspires visions of a perfect beach, beautiful water, and everything that goes along with them.

Twenty-five

Chapter 25. A Timeline of Events in Northwest Florida History Through 2000

"Those who cannot remember the past are condemned to repeat it."
(George Santayana)

Although many of the stories in this book are based on my memory of events my family was involved in, I have tried to present the history of the area as a context for those stories. In researching that history I found it useful to generate a timeline so I could keep track of dates and reduce the time spent returning to references. I also found that I needed to check my memory on many occasions, and so built the personal events into the timeline also. Once the timeline was compiled, I thought it might prove useful to others interested in the development of the area, and so I've included an abridged version of it here. As in the rest of the book, this compilation is centered on Seagrove Beach and extends geographically roughly from Destin and Fort Walton Beach to the west, to Panama City Beach to the east, and to Choctawhatchee Bay to the north.

1000-1200-Fort Walton culture inhabited Walton County

1500 (circa)-European settlers arrived in South Walton County

1513-Ponce De Leon discovered Florida

1559-Don Tristan de Luna y Arellano arrived near Pensacola and attempted to establish a settlement

1559-Great Hurricane

1639-The Chatot Native American people inhabited Walton County

1763-Great Britain obtained title to the Gulf coast

1783-The Treaty of 1783, in which Britain ceded area including what is now Walton County to Spain

1820-Neill McClendon and other settlers arrived in what is now Walton County

1821-The Treaty between Spain and the United States established present boundaries

1822-The Florida Territory was formed

1824-Walton County was formed

1827-First documented settlement in the Panama City area, the John Clark home

1832 (circa)-The Euchee Native American tribe left Walton County

1835 (circa)-The Destin area was settled by New England fisherman Leonard Destin

1856-Law passed making it illegal for Native Americans to live in Florida

1868-John Thomas Brooks arrived in what became known as Camp Walton

1884-John Wesley's home was built in Point Washington, according to homestead documents

1885 (circa)-Grayton Beach was homesteaded by Gray

1887-John Wesley arrived with his family, and filed homestead documents in 1894

1880s-The Point Washington Methodist Church congregation was formed

1888 (circa)-The Point Washington School was built

1890 (circa)-Grayton Beach was founded by Army General William Miller and William Wilson

1890-Plat map of Grayton beach was filed with Walton County

1890s-Washaway House/Hotel was built by Charles Gray, and later owned by Walton Land & Timber

1890 (circa)-Point Washington was founded

1893-William H. Wesley and Katie Strickland married in Point Washington

1893 (circa)-Simeon Strickland and William H. Wesley built a sawmill in Point Washington

1894-The Point Washington Methodist church was built

1895-Wesley mansion construction started; completed circa 1897

1895-Strickland mansion construction also started; completed circa 1897

1903-William H. Wesley homesteaded land at Eastern Lake

1904-President Theodore Roosevelt signed documents granting a homestead in what later became Seagrove Beach

1909-Panama City was incorporated

1913-Land east of Seagrove was homesteaded (Kitrell-Lowery)

1919-W.H. Butler traded property at Inlet Beach for land at Grayton

1920 (circa)-The early Seagrove Hotel was built

1922-Grayton Hotel was built by W.H. Butler

1922-The Seagrove Company bought land and drew a plat map

1923-The Seagrove Company filed a revised plat with Walton County

1926-Great Hurricane of 1926

1928-Storm surge opened the present East Pass in Choctawhatchee Bay

1920s (late)-W.T. Sharpless tried to establish a resort on Long Beach

1929-Alternate date for formation of the Choctawhatchee Bay East Pass

1929-Plat map of Grayton Beach First Addition was filed with Walton County

1929-St. Andrew Bay Bridge opened connecting Panama City Beach with Panama City

1931-Camp Walton became known as Fort Walton

1931-W.T. Sharpless was murdered for trying to collect a tax from beachgoers at Long Beach

1932-Gideon Thomas purchased land for Panama City Beach

1932 (circa)-Long Beach Resort was opened by J.E. Churchwell in Panama City Beach

1933-The Marler Bridge was built, connecting Okaloosa Island to the town of Destin

1936-The St. Joe Paper Company was incorporated

1936-Great Hurricane of 1936

1936-William H. Wesley opened the first Point Washington Post Office

1936-The Gulf Intracoastal Waterway was completed

1936-The Panama City Beach Hotel was built (1935) and Panama City Beach was opened by Gideon Thomas

1937-US highway 98 was completed

1937-The Valparaiso Bombing and Gunnery Base (built in 1935) was designated Eglin Air Force Base

1937-The Grayton Store was built by the Butler family

1937-Coleman Kelly licensed the first sport fishing boat in Destin

1939-Seagrove First Addition plat map was filed by J.R. Moody, president of the Seagrove Company

1940-The Choctawhatchee Bay Bridge on US 331 opened

1940-First systematic archaeological survey of Walton County

1941-Tyndall Air Force Base opened in Panama City

1942-The United States Coast Guard built a station at Grayton Beach

1944-JB-2 flying bomb testing began at Four Mile Point

1946-Snake-A-Torium opened

1948-The first Destin Fishing Rodeo was staged

1948-Plat map of Sea Highland was filed (east of Seagrove Beach)

1949-C.H. McGee, Sr. bought land in Seagrove Beach from J.R. Moody

1949-C.H. McGee, Sr. built Seagrove Beach Real Estate office

1949 (circa)-The forerunner of the Seagrove Village Market was built by C.H. McGee, Sr.

1949-Seagrove Second Addition plat map was filed by C.H. McGee, Sr. & Louise S. McGee

1949-John Fonville bought land from C.H. McGee, Sr.

1950-CR 395 was paved from US 98 to Seagrove

1952-The first duplexes of Seagrove Manor Hotel were built by Paul and Margaret Benedict

1952-The phrase "Miracle Strip" was coined by local newspaper writer Claude Jenkins

1953-The Wesley house was sold to Bronson, with 21 cottages

1952-The forerunner of the Wheelhouse Restaurant was built

1953-City name Fort Walton was changed to Fort Walton Beach

1954-Seagrove Beach developer C.H. McGee, Sr. died

1954-Cube McGee took over development of Seagrove Beach

1955-The Gulfarium opened in Fort Walton Beach

1956-John Fonville moved to Seagrove

1956-Capt. Anderson's restaurant opened in Panama City Beach

1956-Construction began on Scenic Highway 30-A (CR 30-A)

1958-Goofy Golf opened in Fort Walton Beach

1959-Plat map of Seagrove Fourth Addition (with lots along Cube's canal) was filed

1959-Goofy Golf opened in Panama City Beach

1960-The first Hathaway Bridge was constructed in Panama City (replacing the St. Andrew Bay Bridge)

1962-My parents bought their first house in Seagrove Beach

1962-(circa) CR 30-A was completed from Seagrove Beach east to Highway 98

1962-(circa)-The Tombstone Territory and Petticoat Junction Amusement Parks were built in Panama City Beach

1963-My parents bought their Jeep

1963-Lois Maxon bought the Wesley house in Point Washington

1963-The Miracle Strip Amusement Park opened in Panama City Beach

1964-Holiday Inn opened in Panama City Beach

1966-The Top O' the Strip observation tower opened in Panama City Beach

1967-The Lord family bought the Seagrove Manor Hotel from original owners Paul and Margaret Benedict

1968-Lois Maxon donated Eden to the State of Florida; Eden Gardens State Park opened

1968-Grayton Beach State Park opened

1969-Hurricane Camille made landfall along the Mississippi Gulf Coast

1969-My parents bought Hurricane Hall in Seagrove Beach

1970-CR 30-A was completed from Seagrove Beach west to Grayton Beach

1971-The Flowers family bought the Seagrove Manor Hotel

1972-The movie "Frogs" was filmed at Eden Gardens State Park (release date)

1973-Sandestin Resort first opened

1975-Hurricane Eloise hit the panhandle near Fort Walton Beach

1975-Panama City Beach landmark The Hangout was destroyed by Hurricane Eloise

1975-Panama City Beach landmark Skyride was badly damaged by Hurricane Eloise

1975-The Coastal Construction Control Line (CCCL) was established in Walton County

1976-The Seagrove Restaurant was opened by Emory Elkins

1978-*New York Times* columnist Howell Raines coined the phrase "Redneck Riviera"

1979-My parents sold our first house in Seagrove Beach

1979-Hurricane Frederick hit Alabama

1979-The Tombstone Territory Amusement Park was demolished

1981-Seaside was founded

1983-The term "Emerald Coast" was coined by junior high school student Andrew Dier

1984-Seagrove Beach's only high rises were built

1984-Petticoat Junction Amusement Park in Panama City Beach was closed

1989-Old US Highway 98 was closed in Destin

1989-The Grayton Beach Fine Arts Festival began

1992-The former Snake-a-Torium reopened, this time as ZooWorld

1994-The Mid-Bay Bridge opened across Choctawhatchee Bay

1990s-The Village of Baytowne Wharf opened in Sandestin

1995-Hurricane Opal landed near Fort Walton Beach

1995-The Top O' the Strip observation tower was badly damaged by
        Hurricane Opal

1996-Deer Lake State Park opened

1997-Seagrove Beach developer C.H. "Cube" McGee, Jr. died

1997-The movie "Truman Show" was filmed at Seaside

1997-The St. Joe Co. transitioned its business to real estate

1998-The *Shops of Grayton* stores and studios opened

Twenty-six

Chapter 26. Remembering Cube + Babe McGee

"Close friends are truly life's treasures. Sometimes they know us better than we know ourselves. With gentle honesty, they are there to guide and support us, to share our laughter and our tears. Their presence reminds us that we are never really alone." *(Vincent Van Gogh)*

Most stories about Seagrove Beach mention C.H. McGee, Sr. or his son Cube, and almost everyone in the area, at least in past years, had heard of them. But for my family they weren't just people who figured in the development of Seagrove Beach or ran local businesses; for us, they more or less helped define Seagrove. When my parents were looking at property in the area, Cube was one of the realtors who showed them homes. And when they bought their first house, he was the realtor on the sale. It was actually quite a complicated transaction because of financial dealings involving the previous owner and some relatives, and it took months to complete. Cube was there through it all, along with my parents' attorney in Montgomery. And whenever a problem occurred with the house after the purchase, my parents called

Cube McGee fishing on the beach with his pet deer (photo courtesy of the Seagrove Village Market).

Cube for background information or instructions on how to handle it. He also arranged repairs and provided advice on all sorts of things.

I already related how Cube rescued us when we first took our Jeep on the beach, and how he taught me to drive in the sand. There were many more occasions when we called on him for advice, either with the Jeep or with our Boston Whaler. You could always tell when Cube was coming because he had the only pink Jeep on the beach. He also probably had the best traction setup, with very wide rims and smooth (slick) tires. That may not sound like the best tire setup for sand on the beach, but it worked remarkably well.

I remember another occasion, probably when I was in high school, when a friend of mine and I went down from Montgomery for a few days. I don't remember whether we found a problem at the house, or that repairs were being made, or what, but for some reason we couldn't stay at the house for the first night or two. So I contacted Cube or his wife Babe, and Babe immediately insisted that we stay at their house until the problem was solved. They had a nice front guestroom, and she made sure we were well fed while we were there.

Cube was always fishing, and his adventures in the Gulf in his little runabout could probably fill a book. As I recall he kept the boat, probably a 15' or 16' hull, at his house in Seagrove and often launched it from the beach using the pink Jeep. Cube's house can be seen in the upper right section of this book's cover photo. It's the L-shaped house with the light roof. The jeep would be in the carport and the boat in the driveway, if they weren't both on the beach. He would sometimes be out all day, and he must have had an encyclopedic knowledge of the Gulf waters in the area. The photo on the previous page shows Cube fishing on the beach with the McGee's pet deer Bambi. We didn't arrive in the area early enough to see those days, but we have vivid memories of him in his Jeep or boat. Babe was also an avid angler and I remember how excited she got when Cobia were spotted. "The Ling are running" she would say, Ling being another name for Cobia. Cobia are seasonal and at certain times could be spotted from the beach. The bluff at Seagrove Beach provided an excellent vantage point for watching the water. When Babe spotted something or got

Cube and Babe hosting a golf tournament in 1975 (photo by Mary Sullivan, courtesy of the DeFuniak Springs Herald Breeze).

word from a friend, she would grab her surf rod and head for the beach. I don't know how much Babe fished from the boat with Cube, or what her favorite tackle was, but whatever the location and type of tackle, they both loved to fish.

Back in Chapter Seven I introduced the Boston Whaler we used in various bodies of water around Seagrove, including Cube's canal. As I described there, we kept the boat on the trailer at the house during some periods, and at other times in the water in a boathouse. The boat itself was made of fiberglass, which held up pretty well in that environment, but the trailer really took a beating. It was almost always sitting in the salt air, and even when you launched the boat in the bay or a lake the trailer periodically got immersed in water. The worst environment was launching the boat on the beach, when the trailer was doused with salt water. So it's no surprise that eventually the trailer developed lots of rust, not to mention problems with the tires. When my parents finally got ready to sell the first house, where we kept the boat and trailer in a garage, my father decided to just offer both to Cube. He knew it would cost something to make various repairs on the boat and thought he might have to buy a new trailer. And he realized that considering all that Cube had done for us over the years, it would be a nice gesture to give it to him. And, anyway, Cube was better equipped to make the best of it. I was never directly involved in little exchanges like this, but it was easy to see how valuable such a mutual friendship and courtesy could be over the years. In the chapter on Hurricane Hall I related how Cube called my mother one day with information about a possible estate sale involving the house. I don't know how much of that information was public at that point, and my parents' opportunity to buy the house arose solely because Cube McGee thought of them and wanted to be nice or return a favor. And I personally remember that no matter how many projects he did or how well recognized he was in his own world of Seagrove, he always remained courteous and respectful, even to me as a teenager. He was a true gentleman.

The reason I named this chapter Cube + Babe is that I distinctly remember seeing a little heart engraved in a concrete walkway, somewhere in Seagrove Beach, with the inscription Cube + Babe. Cube probably carved it into the freshly poured concrete walk at one of his construction sites. I don't remember the location, but I know it was somewhere in Seagrove, and I hope it remains.

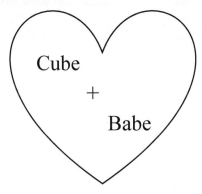

Sketch of the small "Cube + Babe" inscription I remember on a concrete walkway.

Twenty-seven

Chapter 27. New Generations, and the Future of Seagrove Beach

"Each generation imagines itself to be more intelligent than the one that went before it, and wiser than the one that comes after it."
(George Orwell)

In 1990 I moved to the West Coast again to pursue career goals, and by the time Hurricane Opal struck in 1995 I was busy with a family and a new career focus. But I always made time to return to Seagrove and in fact introduced other families and friends to its beauty. In 1998 my son was born, and although that meant even more responsibilities at home, we somehow always managed to get back to Seagrove. My work and education took me to Arizona, and from there we both flew and drove to Seagrove. Soon after, I became involved with NASA space programs, and since some of that work occurred in Florida, I was usually able to combine work trips with time off at Seagrove. Rocket launches took place at Cape Canaveral for unmanned missions and at Cape Kennedy for manned missions on the space shuttle. Seagrove Beach made a nice stopping point for a trip to Cocoa Beach for a launch. The Atlantic beaches aren't as pretty as the

Emerald Coast, but they're really good for launching rockets. This photo shows the launch of the Delta rocket for the Mars Polar Lander mission in 1998. I helped design and build the science camera for this Mars mission.

Launch of the Delta rocket for the Mars Polar Lander mission in 1998 (NASA photo).

Hurricane Hall served dual duty as a rental home through most of the summer and in the winter, and a family retreat for a few choice weeks each year, mostly in the spring and fall. Although this book only covers up to around the year 2000, I have included the photo below showing my son at about the age of four, heading down the steps for some beach time in the fall.

The author and his son heading to the beach.

Seagrove Beach has of course continued to develop and change with each passing year. In many ways C.H. McGee, Sr.'s vision of a community has been realized, and his rules and restrictions have mostly helped make it a tidy and pleasant community. For most residents, the advertisement written on the side of his first real estate office "A good investment; Fine place to live" has been true. The original slow acceptance by buyers of Seagrove's resources and opportunities has given way to periods of rapid and even explosive growth. For context, the following aerial photo was taken in 2012 from almost the same position as the cover photo, and shows the growth and changes that occurred over a period of about 30 years. No one knows what the future will bring, but let's hope nature is kind to this little strip of beach, this wonderful place that to my family has always been simply Seagrove.

Aerial photo of Seagrove Beach taken in 2012 from about the same position as the cover photo (photo courtesy of Alice Forrester).

Acknowledgments

I would like to thank Alice Forrester for encouraging me to continue this project, for providing several unique photos, and for reading the manuscript. Jill Berkowitz Provan edited the manuscript, and provided many useful design suggestions and sources of information. Flip Spann provided access to a library of photos that enhanced many important areas. I thank Maunsel White for providing photos of Mary Bruns' paintings and granting permission for them to be used. Dr. James Poteet provided background on art in Seagrove, details on the Shops of Grayton, and permission to use some of his work. Brenda Rees introduced me to several important aspects of the early history of Walton County and provided several references. Bitsy Nelson provided documentation and references on the area. Harvey H. Jackson III provided information and connected me with other sources in the area. Frances Kelley provided information on the Point Washington area. Tim Hollis read the manuscript and provided comments. Jim Stephens provided vital information about several photos my family had taken. The Seagrove Village Market provided several archival photos. The *DeFuniak Springs Herald Breeze* newspaper granted permission to use some archival photos they had published. Steve Fielding at Northwest Florida State College Library provided valuable help in researching references. Finally, I thank my sister Sarah, Sally to us, for sharing the back seat of the Buick station wagon with me on all those drives to the beach when my parents were locating what would become our second home.

Bibliography

Note: Personal communications are inserted in the text., and not included here.

"About Dewey Destin's Harborside Restaurant" Retrieved from http://www.destinseafood .com/DestinHarbor/About/.

American Society Of Mechanical Engineers. "The JEEP MB, An International Historic Mechanical Engineering Landmark." New York, NY, American Society Of Mechanical Engineers, 1991.

"ArtsQuest Fine Arts Festival." Retrieved from https://www.artweeksouthwalton.com/artsquest/.

Associated Press. "Where They Really Knew Popeye and Co." *The New York Times,* January 18, 2004.

Baughman, James Keir. *Villages By An Emerald Sea: True Tales Of the Early Years.* Baughman Literary Group, 2003.

Bernstein, Fred A. "Seaside at 25: Troubles in Paradise." *The New York Times,* December 9, 2005.

Berwald, Juli. *Spineless: The Science of Jellyfish and the Art of Growing a Backbone* New York, NY, Riverhead Books, 2017.

"Bruns, Mary Bryan." Retrieved from sowal.com/forum.

Bush, David M., et.al. *Living On the Edge Of the Gulf: The West Florida and Alabama Coast.* Durham, NC, Duke University Press, 2001.

Carswell, E.W. *Washington, Florida's Twelfth County.* E.W. Carswell, 1991.

Chamberlain, Jo. "Meet the Jeep: The United States Army's Answer to Schick Ie gruber's Panzer Divisions." *Scientific American.* January, 1942.

Choctawhatchee Basin Alliance. *Coastal Dune Lakes Of Walton County.* Retrieved from https:// www. basinalliance.org.

Cox, Isaac Joslin. *The West Florida Controversy, 1798-1813; a study in American diplomacy.* Baltimore, The Johns Hopkins Press, 1918.

Davis, Jack E. *The Gulf: The Making of An American Sea.* New York, NY, Liveright/W. W. Norton, 2017.

Davis, Richard A. Jr. *Beaches Of the Gulf Coast.* College Station, TX, Texas A&M University Press, 2014.

Deer Lake State Park. Florida State Parks   Retrieved from https://www.floridastateparks. org/park/deer-lake.

Destin Chamber Of Commerce. "History Of Destin & Its White Sand." Retrieved from http:// www.destinchamber.com/ history-of-destin.

Dixon, Wendy O. "Saving Grayton Beach." *Emerald Coast Magazine.* August, 2009.

Duncan, Wilbur H. *The Smithsonian Guide To Seaside Plants Of the Gulf and Atlantic Coasts from Louisiana To Massachusetts, exclusive of lower peninsular Florida.* Washington, D.C., Smithsonian Institution Press, 1987.

Dunlop, Bath. "In Florida, a New Emphasis on Design." *The New York Times,* December 9, 2001.

"Eglin Air Force Base History." Retrieved from http://www.eglin.af. mil/library/factsheets/factsheet.asp?id=6061.

Encyclopedia Britannica, Inc. *The New Encyclopedia Britannica.* Chicago, University Of Chicago, 1988.

Encyclopedia Britannica, Inc. (1988). Crepuscular Rays. *The New Encyclopedia Britannica.* Chicago, University Of Chicago, Retrieved from https:// www.britannica.com/ science/crepuscular-ray.

Etheridge, Denise. "Humor Through Art." *Walton Sun.* December 19. 1998.

Farjon, Aljos. *A Handbook of the World's Conifers.* Leiden-Boston, Brill Academic Publishers, 2017.

Feininger, Andreas. *The Color Photo Book.* Englewood Cliffs, NJ, Prentice-Hall, 1969.

"The Filming Of Frogs." *Holiday Inn Magazine,* October, 1972.

"Florida Attractions Timeline." Retrieved from http:// www.lostparks.com/timeline.html.

Florida Department of Environmental Protection. *The Homeowner's Guide To The Coastal Construction Control Line Program.* Tallahassee, FL, Florida Department of Environmental Protection, 2006.

Florida Fish and Wildlife Conservation Commission. "Choctawhatchee beach mouse." Retrieved from http://myfwc.com/wildlifehabitats/imperiled/profiles/mamm als/choctawhatchee-beach-mouse/.

FLOWERS v. SEAGROVE BEACH, INC., 479 So.2d 841, (District Court of Appeal of Florida, First District 1985).

Funding Universe. "St. Joe Paper Company History." Retrieved from http://www.fundinguniverse.com/company-histories/st-joe-paper-company.

Galvan, Abraham. "Destin's forgotten history." *Northwest Florida Daily News,* July 11, 2017.

Garman, Valerie. "Panama City Beach tourism transformed over 75 years." *Panama City News-Herald,* September 16, 2012.

"Gideon Thomas' Vision for Panama City Beach Comes True." *Memorable Moments In Bay County History.* October 1, 2013. Retrieved from http://www.baycounty100 .com/Moments-Bay-County-Archive.aspx.

Grayton Beach History. Retrieved from http://www.graytonbeach.com/grayton-beach-history/.

Griffin, Pam. "TASTE OF YESTERDAY: Destin remembers restaurants from days gone by." *Destin Log,* September 5, 2013.

Hershenson, Maurice. *The Moon Illusion.* Hillsdale, NJ. Lawrence Erlbaum Associates, 1989.

Hollis, Tim. *Dixie Before Disney: 100 Years of Roadside Fun.* Jackson. MS. University Press of Mississippi. 2004.

Hollis, Tim. *Florida's Miracle Strip: From Redneck Riviera to Emerald Coast* Jackson, MS, University Press of Mississippi, 2004.

Hurricane Eloise, National Weather Service Retrieved from https://www.weather.gov/mob/Eloise.

Hurricane Opal, National Weather Service Retrieved from https://www.weather.gov/mob/opal.

Jackson, Harvey H., III, *The Rise and Decline Of the Redneck Riviera, An Insider's History Of the Florida-Alabama Coast.* Athens, Georgia, The University Of Georgia Press, 2013.

Jackson, Roy A. *Historic Highway Bridges Of Florida.* Tallahassee, FL, Environmental Management Office, Florida Department Of Transportation, 2004.

Kaplan, Eugene H. *A Field Guide To Southeastern and Caribbean Seashores* Boston, MA, Houghton Mifflin Company, 1988.

Kaufman, Lloyd and Irvin Rock. "The Moon Illusion" *Scientific American.* 1962.

"The Killing Of Walter Sharpless." July 1, 2013. Retrieved from http://www.baycounty100 .com/Moments-Bay-County-Archive.aspx.

Koons, Jennifer. "Supreme Court Justices Hear Arguments in High-Stakes Takings Case." *The New York Times,* December 2, 2009.

Lindsay, J.F., Criswell, D.R., Criswell, T.L. & Criswell, B.S. "Sound-producing dune and beach sands", *GSA Bulletin.* vol. 87. no. 3. 1976.

Livingston, R.J. *Eutrophication Processes In Coastal Systems: Origin and Succession of Plankton Blooms and Effects on Secondary Production In Gulf Coast Estuaries.* Boca Raton, FL, CRC Press, 2000.

Livingston, Robert J. *Trophic Organization in Coastal Systems.* Boca Raton, FL, CRC Press, 2003.

McCoy-Root, Julie. "Grayton Fine Arts Festival to feature accomplished artist." *Destin Log,* May, 1991.

McDonald, Walter H. *Highways Of Florida* Tallahassee, State Road Department Of Florida, 1937.

McKinnon, John L. *History of Walton County* Atlanta, GA, The Byrd Printing Company, 1968.

Merkel, Diane. "The W.H. Wesley Family of Point Washington." in *Walton Relations.* DeFuniak Springs, FL, Walton County Genealogy Society, March, 2015.

Milanich, Jerald T. *Archaeology Of Pre-Columbian Florida.* Gainesville, FL, University Press Of Florida, 1994.

Military History Now. "What the Hell is a "Jeep"? — How Did America's Famous Military 4×4 Get Its Name?" November 27, 2015. Retrieved from http://militaryhistorynow.com.

"'Miracle Strip' Tag Official For This Area." *Playground News.* March 22, 1956.

Morang, Andrew. *A Study Of Geologic and Hydraulic Processes At East Pass, Destin, Florida, Volume I Main Text and Appendices A and B.* Vicksburg, MI, Coastal Engineering Research Center, Department Of the Army, Waterways Experiment Station, Corps of Engineers, 1992.

Mormino, Gary R. *Land of Sunshine, State of Dreams: A Social History of Modern Florida.* Gainesville, FL, University Press of Florida, 2008.

Morris, Allen Covington and Joan Perry Morris. *Florida Handbook.* Peninsular Publishing Company, 2007.

Morton, Julia F. "Wild Plants For Survival In South Florida." Florida State Horticultural Society, 1961.

Mosher, Molly. "A Poteet Soiree." *Walton Sun.* June 30, 2012.

"Destin, Florida: Museum of the Sea and Indian (Gone)." Retrieved from https://www.roadsideamerica.com/tip/2856.

National Climatic Data Center. *Hurricane Opal Technical Report 95-02*. National Climatic Data Center, 1995.

National Hurricane Center. *Hurricanes In History*. National Hurricane Center Retrieved from http:// www.nhc.noaa.gov/ outreach/history/.

Nori, Franco, Paul Sholtz, Michael Bretz._ "Booming Sand"_*Scientific American.* Vol. 277, No. 3, September, 1997.

O'Donovan, Michael and Robin Rowan, *Florida's Northwest: First Places Wild Places Favorite Places.* Pensacola, FL, Terra Nova Publishing, 2005.

Owen, Joyce. "Paradise Found at Eden Gardens." *Emerald Coast Magazine.* October, 2008.

"Panama City Beach Attractions –A Nostalgic Trip into the Past." Retrieved from http://visitpcfla.com/article/panama-city-beach-attractions-%E2%80%93-nostalgic-trip-past.

"Panama City Beach Celebrates 80 Years." *Panama City Living,* May 4, 2016.

"Panama City Salutes "Frogs" World Premiere." *Panama City News-Herald,* March 23, 1972.

Pierce, R.H. and M.S. Henry. "Harmful algal toxins of the Florida red tide (Karenia brevis): natural chemical stressors in South Florida coastal ecosystems." *Ecotoxicology.* Vol. 17, No. 7, October, 2008.

Proctor, Niels and Martha Monroe. "Common Pines of Florida." Gainesville, FL, University Of Florida IFAS Extension, 2016.

Public Ledger, Walton County map, in *Philadelphia Public Ledger's Unrivaled Atlas of the World.* Chicago, Rand McNally & Co., 1900, Retrieved from http://fcit.usf.edu/ florida/maps/pages/ 1700/f1793/f1793.htm.

Raines, Howell. "Todd and Stabler Offseason Game: Living It Up on 'Redneck Riviera'." *The New York Times,* June 21, 1978.

Rees, Brenda. "A pompano fishing story from Grayton Beach," April 18, 2016, Retrieved from https ://www.waltonoutdoors.com /a-pompano-fishing-story-from-grayton-beach/.

Ross, D.A. *Introduction to Oceanography.* New York, NY, HarperCollins, 1995.

Ross, Ken. "Ken'Spen." *Playground News.* May 29, 1970.

Rucker, Brian R. *Treasures Of the Panhandle, A Journey Through West Florida.* Gainesville, FL, University Press Of Florida, 2011.

Ruth, B., and L. R. Handley. "Choctawhatchee Bay" in *Seagrass Status and Trends in the Northern Gulf of Mexico: 1940– 2002.* edited by L. Handley, D. Altsman, and R. DeMay, U.S. Geol. Surv. Sci. Invest. Rep., 2006.

Scenic 30-A Corridor Advocacy Group. "Scenic 30-A Corridor Management Plan." Tallahassee, FL, Kimley-Horn and Associates, Inc., 2007.

Sinko, Peggy Tuck and Kathryn Ford Thorne. *Atlas of Historical County Boundaries: Florida.* ed. John H. Long. New York, Charles Scribner's Sons, 1997.

Sobel, Michael I. *Light.* Chicago, IL, University Of Chicago Press.1987.

South Walton Three Arts Alliance. *The Way We Were, Recollections Of South Walton Pioneers* Santa Rosa Beach. Florida, South Walton Three Arts Alliance, 1997.

South Walton Three Arts Alliance. *Of Days Gone By, Reflections Of South Walton County, Florida* Santa Rosa Beach, Florida, South Walton Three Arts Alliance, 1999.

"South Walton thru the decades." Retrieved from https://www.visitsouthwalton.com/tips-trips/south-walton-through-the-decades.

State Library and Archives of Florida, Florida Memory-Florida Photographic Collection, Tallahassee, Fl, Florida Department of State.

Stevenson, Carrie. "Resurrection Ferns." Retrieved from http://nwdistrict.ifas.ufl.edu/hort /2013/09/02/resurrection-ferns/.

United States. Army Corps of Engineers. *Draft Environmental Impact Statement, East Pass Channel, Choctawhatchee Bay, (Maintenance Dredging), Okaloosa County, Florida.* 1976 (also listed as 1973).

United States Department of Agriculture. "Plant Fact Sheet: Sea Oats." United States Department of Agriculture, Retrieved from https://plants.usda.gov/factsheet/pdf/fs_unpa.pdf.

United States Department of Commerce, Environmental Science Services Administration. *Hurricane Camille, A Report to the Administrator.* Washington, DC, United States Department of Commerce, 1969.

United States Department of the Interior Geological Survey. *Topographical Maps* (various). Washington, DC, United States Geological Survey, various dates.

United States Geological Survey. *Aerial photographs of Walton County.* Various flight and frame numbers and scales. Washington, DC, United States Geological Survey, 1942, Retrieved from http://ufdc.ufl.edu/aerials/results/?t=walton county.

University Of Arizona Accelerator Mass Spectrometry Lab. "Radiocarbon dating." Retrieved from https://ams.arizona.edu/radiocarbon.

Vasquez, Savannah. "William T. Marler: The man behind the bridge." *Northwest Florida Daily News,* November 9, 2015.

Vignoles, Charles Blacker. *Observations Upon the Floridas.* New York, NY, E. Bliss & E. White, 1823.

Walsh, Roberta A. 1994. Uniola paniculata. In: Fire Effects Information System, [Online]. United States Department of Agriculture, Forest Service, Rocky Mountain Research Station, Fire Sciences Laboratory (Producer). Retrieved from https://www.fs.fed.us/ database/feis/plants/ graminoid/unipan/all.html.

Walton County, Florida, Clerk Of Courts. Deeds, real property, various. DeFuniak Springs, FL, Walton County, Florida, Clerk Of Courts. Retrieved from http://orsearch.clerkofcourts. co.walton.fl.us/.

Walton County, Florida, Clerk Of Courts. Plat maps, various. DeFuniak Springs, FL, Walton County, Florida, Clerk Of Courts. Retrieved from http://orsearch.clerkofcourts. co.walton.fl.us/.

Weeks, J.D. *Panama City - Postcard History Series.* Charleston, SC, Arcadia Publishing, 2005.

Wesley, Gene. "Walton What?" (Letter to the Editor), *Walton Sun,* February 19, 2005.

Wesley, William H. III *Land Of Eden, Memories and Thoughts About Living In This Land* Indianapolis, IN, Dog Ear Publishing, 2008.

"What Disney's city of the future, built to look like the past, says about the present." *The Economist.* December 24, 2016.

Wheeler, Deborah. "Days gone by in Seagrove: Remembering Seagrove founder, Cube McGee." *Walton Sun,* September 13, 2003.

Wheeler, Deborah. "Wheel House Restaurant burns in early morning fire." *Walton Sun,* July 29, 2005.

Wheeler, Deborah. "Eden State Park is a must see bit of history." *Walton Sun,* September 29, 2016.

"Who owns 'Emerald Coast'?" *Northwest Florida Daily News,* June 29, 2011.

Williams, Dwight. "Rags to Riches Regatta Returns To Grayton Beach." June 7, 2014. Retrieved from http://sowal.com /story/rags-to-riches-regatta-returns-to-grayton-beach.

Wolfgram, Zandra. "Sandestin Is 40!". *Emerald Coast Magazine.* 2013.

Womack, Marlene. "A History of Bay County." *Panama City News-Herald,* May 15, 2013.

Worth, John. "September 19, 1559: A Hurricane That Changed History." WUWF Radio broadcast, September 19, 2017.

Ziewitz, Kathryn, and June Wiaz. *Green Empire: The St. Joe Company and the Remaking of Florida's Panhandle.* Gainesville, Florida: University Press of Florida, 2004.

.

Index

fern, resurrection, 76

Florida Department Of Environmental Protection, 32, 33, 34

Florida Panhandle, 4, 1, 3, 42, 45, 49, 57, 70, 86, 104, 168

Flowers, Marie S., 28

Fonville, John, 15, 144, 176, 177

Forest St, 21

Forest St., 21, 68

Fort Walton, 3, 12, 43, 87, 94, 96, 97, 104, 119, 121, 126, 127, 162, 163, 169, 171, 173, 174, 175, 177, 178, 179

Fort Walton Beach, 12, 87, 104, 121, 126, 127, 162, 163, 169, 171, 173, 177, 178, 179

Frogs (movie), 113, 114, 115, 178, 193, 196

Fuller Lake, 44

gibbon, 92

Goofy Golf, 127, 128, 177

Gray, Charles T., 4, 101

Grayton Beach, 4, 5, 10, 13, 14, 36, 45, 57, 68, 80, 83, 84, 101, 104, 105, 121, 122, 123, 124, 129, 131, 152, 153, 154, 155, 156, 170, 174, 175, 176, 178, 179, 190, 192, 194, 195, 197

Grayton Beach Fine Arts Festival, 153, 154, 155, 178

Grayton Beach State Park, 83, 84, 129, 178

Grayton Hotel, 104, 121, 122, 175

Grayton Store, 122, 123, 176

Great Britain, 4, 174

green hill, 5

Grove St., 21, 68

Gulf Coast, 4, 192, 195

Gulf Of Mexico, 27, 28, 32, 42, 46, 47, 51, 86, 104, 126, 169

gull, 91

Halley's Comet, 7, 143, 146, 149, 150

Hang Out, 118, 119, 124

Hobie Cat, 23

Hogtown Bayou, 3

Holiday Inn, 12, 177, 193

Horseshoe Bayou, 43

hurricane, 100, 101, 102

Hurricane Eloise, 104, 105, 122, 124, 128, 178, 194

New York Times, 170, 178, 191, 192, 194, 196

Northwest Florida, 8, 71, 100, 169, 173, 190, 193, 198, 199

oak, live, 71

oak, scrub, 64, 71, 93, 151, 159, 170

Okaloosa County, 3, 34, 96, 162, 171, 176, 198

Outboard Marine Corporation, 95

Panama City, 7, 43, 46, 49, 57, 98, 99, 104, 105, 115, 117, 118, 119, 121, 124, 127, 128, 134, 169, 171, 173, 174, 175, 176, 177, 178, 193, 196, 199

Panama City Beach, 104, 105, 117, 118, 119, 124, 127, 128, 169, 173, 175, 176, 177, 178, 193, 196

Panhandle, Florida, 4, 12, 13, 42, 71, 102, 104, 127, 163, 169, 178

Pensacola, 47, 96, 97, 100, 101, 127, 163, 169, 171, 174, 196

Petticoat Junction, 128, 177, 178

Playground Daily News, 169, 195, 197

Point Washington, 7, 3, 4, 7, 21, 36, 37, 40, 43, 71, 75, 76, 111, 122, 123, 174, 175, 176, 177, 190

Pompano, 86

Ponce de Leon, 3

Port St. Joe, 71

Portuguese Man of War, 88, 89

Poteet, Dr. Jim, 136, 153, 154, 155, 156

pottery, 3, 64, 68, 69, 153, 160

Powell Lake, 44

radiocarbon dating, 69

Rags to Riches Regatta, 23, 24, 199

Railroad Vine, 74

Raines, Howell, 170, 178

Red Snapper, 86

red tide, 78, 196

Redneck Riviera, 170, 178, 194, 196

restrictions, 26, 62, 135, 188

Roosevelt, Theodore, 6

Rosemary Beach, 10

Russ, James L., 6

Russ's Hammock, 6

Made in the USA
Monee, IL
06 December 2019